THE
CASE FOR
COPYRIGHT
REFORM

CHRISTIAN ENGSTRÖM MEP
& RICK FALKVINGE

The Greens | European Free Alliance
in the European Parliament

This book is published by Pirate MEP Christian Engström
with support from the Greens/EFA-group in the European Parliament.

ISBN: 978-1-4716-7178-4

Printed by Lulu.com

This book also can be found as an e-book with active links at
www.copyrightreform.eu

Contct details:
Christian Engström: christianengstrom.wordpress.com
Rick Falkvinge: falkvinge.net
Greens/EFA in the EP: www.greens-efa.eu

Contents

Chapter 1

There Is A Better Way

Today's copyright legislation is out of balance, and out of tune with the times. It has turned an entire generation of young people into criminals in the eyes of the law, in a futile attempt at stopping technological development. Yet file sharing has continued to grow exponentially. Neither propaganda, fear tactics, nor ever harsher laws have been able to stop the development.

It is impossible to enforce the ban against non-commercial file sharing without infringing on fundamental human rights. As long as there are ways for citizens to communicate in private, they will be used to share copyrighted materials. The only way to even try to limit file sharing is to remove the right to private communication. In the last decade, this is the direction that copyright enforcement legislation has moved in, under pressure from big business lobbyists who see their monopolies under threat. We need to reverse this trend to safeguard fundamental rights.

At the same time, we want a society where culture flourishes, and where artists and creative people have a chance to make a living as cultural workers. Fortunately, there is no contradiction between file sharing and culture. This is something we know from a decade's experience of massive file sharing on the Internet.

In the economic statistics, we can see that household spending on culture and entertainment is slowly increasing year by year. If we spend less money on buying CDs, we spend more on something else, such as going to live concerts. This is great news for artists. An artist will typically get 5-7% of the revenues from a CD, but 50% of the revenues from a concert. The record companies lose out, but this is only because they are no longer adding any value.

It may well be that it will become more difficult to make money within some parts of the cultural sector, but if so, it will become easier in some others – including new ones, that we have not even imagined so far. But as long as the total household spending on culture continues to be on the same level or rising, nobody can claim that artists in general will have anything to lose from a reformed copyright.

Should this also have the side effect of loosening up some of the grip that the big distributors have over cultural life, then so much the better for both artists and consumers.

When public libraries were introduced in Europe 150 years ago, the book publishers were very much opposed to this. The argument they used was the same one that is being used today in the file sharing debate: If people could get access to books for free, authors would not be able to make a living, and no new books would be written.

We now know that the arguments against public libraries were wrong. It quite obviously did not lead to a situation where no new books were written, and it did not make it impossible for authors to earn money from writing. On the contrary, free access to culture proved to be not only a boon to society at large, but also turned out to be beneficial to authors.

The Internet is the most fantastic public library that has ever been created. It means that everybody, including people with limited economic means, has access to all the world's culture just a mouse-click away. This is a positive development that we should embrace and applaud.

The Pirate Party has a clear and positive agenda to end criminalization of the young generation, and provide the foundation for a diverse and sustainable cultural sector in the Internet age. We invite all political groups to copy our ideas.

Sharing is caring.

Chapter 2

A Constructive Proposal For Copyright Reform

The Pirate Party does not want to abolish copyright; we want to reform it. We want to keep copyright for commercial purposes, but we want to set all non-commercial copying and use free.

This reform is urgent, as the attempts to enforce today's ban on non-commercial sharing of culture between private citizens are threatening fundamental rights, such as the right to private communication, freedom of information, and even the right to due process.

File sharing is when two private individuals send ones and zeros to each other. The only way to even try to limit file sharing, is to introduce surveillance of everybody's private communication. There is no way to separate private messages from copyrighted material without opening the messages and checking the contents. Gone is the postal secret, the right to communicate in private with your lawyer or your web-cam flirt, or your whistle-blower protection if you want to give a sensitive story to a journalist.

We are not prepared to give up our fundamental rights to enforce today's copyright. The right to privacy is more important than the right of big media companies to continue to make money in the same way as before, because the latter right does not even exist.

Today's copyright also prevents or restricts many new and exciting cultural expressions. Sampled music on MySpace, remixes on YouTube, or why not a Wikipedia filled with lots of pictures and music in the articles? Copyright legislation says no.

The copyright laws must either be reformed or abolished outright. The Pirate Party advocates the reform alternative.

We want to set all non-commercial copying and use free, and we want to shorten the commercial protection time. But we want to keep the commercial exclusivity in a way that allows most business models that are viable today to continue to work.

Our proposal can be summarized in six points:

• Moral Rights Unchanged

We propose no changes at all to the moral right of the author to be recognized as the author.

Nobody should be allowed to claim that they are ABBA, or have written all of Paul McCartney's songs, unless they actually are or have. To the extent that this is a real world problem, it should still be illegal to do so. "Give credit where credit is due" is a good maxim that everybody agrees with.

• Free Non-Commercial Sharing

Until twenty years ago, copyright hardly concerned ordinary people. The rules about exclusivity of the production of copies were aimed at commercial actors, who had the means to, for example, print books or press records.

Private citizens who wanted to copy a poem and send to their loved one, or copy a record to cassette and give it to a friend, did not have to worry about being in breach of copyright. In practice, anything you had the technical means to do as a normal person, you could do without risk of any punishment.

But today, copyright has evolved to a position where it imposes serious restrictions on what ordinary citizens can do in their every-day lives. As technological progress has made it easier for ordinary people to enjoy and share culture, copyright legislation has moved in the opposite direction.

We want to restore copyright to its origins, and make absolutely clear that it only regulates copying for commercial purposes. To share copies, or otherwise spread or make use of use somebody else's copyrighted work, should never be prohibited if it is done by private individuals without a profit motive. Peer-to-peer file sharing is an example of such an activity that should be legal.

• 20 Years Of Commercial Monopoly

Much of today's entertainment industry is built on the commercial exclusivity of copyrighted works. This, we want to preserve. But today's protection times – life plus 70 years – are absurd. No investor would even look at a business case where the time to pay-back was that long.

We want to shorten the protection time to something that is reasonable from both society's and an investor's point of view, and propose 20 years from publication.

• Registration After 5 Years

Today, works that are still in copyright, but where it is impossible or difficult to locate the rights owner, are a major problem. The majority of these works have little or no commercial value, but since they are still covered by copyright, they cannot be reused or distributed because there is nobody to ask for permission.

Copyright protection should be given automatically like it is today to newly published works, but rights owners who want to continue to exercise their commercial exclusivity of a work beyond the first 5 years after publication should be required to register the right, in such a way that it can be found by a diligent search of public rights databases. This will solve the orphan works problem.

• Free Sampling

Today's ever more restrictive copyright legislation and practice is a major obstacle to musicians, film makers, and other artists who want to create new works by reusing parts of existing works. We want to change this by introducing clear exceptions and limitations to allow remixes and parodies, as well as quotation rights for sound and audiovisual material modeled after the quotation rights that already exist for text.

• A Ban on DRM

DRM is an acronym for "Digital Rights Management", or "Digital Restrictions Management". The term is used to denote a number of different technologies that all aim to restrict consumers' and citizens' ability use and copy works, even when they have a legal right to do so.

It must always be legal to circumvent DRM restrictions, and we should consider introducing a ban in the consumer rights legislation on DRM technologies that restrict legal uses of a work. There is no point in having our parliaments introduce a balanced and reasonable copyright legislation, if at the same time we allow the big multinational corporations to write their own laws, and enforce them through technical means.

This is, in essence, what the Swedish Pirate Party proposes, and the position on copyright that the Greens/EFA group in the European Parliament adopted in September 2011.

The proposal is completely in line with ideas that have been voiced in the international debate, such as Lawrence Lessig's *Free Culture* or Yochai Benkler's *The Wealth of Networks*. These ideas have been thoroughly discussed for at least a decade, both by academics and the Internet community.

"But how will the artists get paid, if file sharing is set free?" is the question that always comes up in the discussion.

Well, "how" is not really for us to say as politicians. To find a business model that works is up to the individual entrepreneur, in the cultural sector just as in any other industry. But we are certain that the cultural sector as a whole will continue to do well, as demonstrated by economic statistics from more than a decade of rampant file sharing. There is no conflict between file sharing and the production of new culture, quite the opposite. Our proposal is good for the artists, both from a creative and an economic point of view.

But the issue is bigger than that. This is about what kind of society we want.

The Internet is the greatest thing that has happened to mankind since the printing press, and quite possibly a lot greater. The Pirate Bay, Wikipedia, and the Arab Spring have made headlines as dedicated people have put the new technology to work to spread culture, knowledge, and democracy, respectively. And we have only seen the beginning.

But at this moment of fantastic opportunity, copyright is putting obstacles in the way of creativity, and copyright enforcement threatens fundamental rights, including the right to private communication, the right to receive and impart information without interference by public authority regardless of frontiers, the right to due process, and the principle of proportionality when punishments are handed out.

We need to change the direction that copyright legislation is going in, in order to protect our fundamental rights. No business model is worth more than the right to private communication and freedom of information.

Copyright needs to be reformed urgently.

Chapter 3

Copyright Enforcement Threatens Fundamental Rights

The Right To Talk In Private

Six years ago, when I, Rick Falkvinge, founded the Swedish and first Pirate Party, we set three pillars for our policy: shared culture, free knowledge, and fundamental privacy. These were themes that were heard as ideals in respected activist circles. I had a gut feeling that they were connected somehow, but it would take another couple months for me to connect the dots between the right to the fundamental liberty of privacy and the right to share culture.

The connection was so obvious once you had made it, it's still one of our best points: *Today's level of copyright cannot coexist with the right to communicate in private.*

If I send you an e-mail, that e-mail may contain a piece of music. If we are in a video chat, I may drop a copyrighted video clip there for both of us to watch. The only way to detect this, in order to enforce today's level of copyright, is to eliminate the right to private correspondence. That is, to eavesdrop on all the ones and zeros going to and from all computers.

There is no way to allow the right to private correspondence for some type of content, but not for other types. You must break the seal and analyze the contents to sort it into allowed and disallowed. At that point, the seal is broken. Either there is a seal on everything, or on nothing.

So we are at a crossroads. We, as a society, can say that copyright is the most important thing we have, and give up the right to talk in private. Either that, or we say that the right to private correspondence has greater value, even though such correspondence can be used to transfer copyrighted works. There is no middle ground.

What has become clear recently is the level of understanding of this within the copyright industry, and how they persistently try to eradicate the right to private correspondence in order to safeguard current disputed levels of copyright. A cable leaked by WikiLeaks in December 2010 outlined a checklist given to the Swedish government with demands from the US copyright industry, IIPA. The US Embassy was quite appreciative of how the Swedish justice department was "fully on board" and had made considerable progress on the demands against its own citizens, in favor of the US copyright industry.

In those demands were pretty much every Big Brother law enacted in the past several years. Data retention, Ipred, three-strikes, police access to IP records for petty crimes, abolishment of the mere conduit messenger immunity, everything was in there.

The copyright industry is actively driving a Big Brother society, as it understands that this path is the only way to save copyright. It's time to throw that industry out of the legislative process.

One of the primary demands of the Pirate Party is that the same laws that apply offline, should also apply online. This is an entirely reasonable thing to demand. The Internet is not a special case, but part of reality. The problems appear when an obsolete but powerful industry realizes that this just and equal application of laws means that they can't enforce their distribution monopoly any longer.

To understand the absurdity of the copyright industry's demands, we must pause and consider which rights we take absolutely for granted in the analog world. These are rights that already apply in the digital part of reality as well, but are somehow hidden in a legal game of hide-and-seek.

Let's look at what rights I have when I communicate through analog channels with somebody – using paper, a pen, an envelope, and a stamp. The same rights should apply when using a digital communications channel instead, at least theoretically, since the law doesn't differentiate between methods of communication. Unfortunately for the copyright industry, the enforcement of our rights online would mean that the copyright monopoly becomes utterly unenforceable, so the copyright industry is now attacking these fundamental rights on every level. But that doesn't mean our rights aren't there.

When I write a letter to somebody, I and I alone choose whether I identify myself in the letter inside the envelope, on the outside of the envelope, both, or neither. It is completely my prerogative whether I choose to communicate anonymously or not. This is a right we have in analog communications and in law; it is perfectly reasonable to demand that the law applies online as well.

When I write a letter to somebody, nobody has the right to intercept the letter in transit, break its seal and examine its contents unless I am under formal, individual and prior suspicion of a specific crime. In that case, law enforcement (and only them) may do this. Of course, I am never under any obligation to help anybody open and interpret my letters. It is perfectly reasonable to demand that this applies online as well.

When I write a letter to somebody, no third party has the right to alter the contents of the letter in transit or deny its delivery. Isn't it perfectly reasonable to demand that this applies online as well?

When I write a letter to somebody, nobody has the right to stand at the mailbox and demand that they log all my communications: who I am communicating with, when, and for how long. Again, to demand that this applies online as well would only be logical.

When I write a letter to somebody, the mailman carrying that letter to its recipient is never responsible for what I have written. He has messenger immunity. And yes, it is perfectly reasonable to demand that this applies online as well.

All of these fundamental rights are under systematic attack by the copyright industry. They are suing ISPs and demanding that they install wiretapping and censoring equipment in the middle of their switching racks. They are constantly gnawing at messenger immunity (mere conduit and common carrier principle), they are demanding the authority to identify people who communicate, they want the authority to deny us our right to exercise fundamental rights at all, and they have the nerve to suggest censorship to safeguard the distribution monopoly.

All of the above stems from the fact that any digital communications channel that can be used for private correspondence, can also always be used to transfer digitizations of copyrighted works – and you can't tell which is which without giving the copyright industry the right to break the seal of private correspondence, which is a right the Pirate Party is not prepared to surrender.

These are civil liberties that our forefathers fought, bled, and died to give us. It is beyond obscene that an obsolete middleman industry is demanding that we give up our rights to preserve an entertainment monopoly, and demanding more powers than we are even giving the police to catch real criminals. Then again, this is nothing new.

When photocopiers arrived in the 1960s, book publishers tried to have them banned on the grounds that they could be used to copy books which would then be sent in the mail. Everybody told the publishers tough luck: While the copyright monopoly is still valid, they have no right to break the seal on communications just to look for copyright infringements, so they can't do anything about it. That still applies offline. It is perfectly reasonable to demand that it applies online as well.

The copyright industry sometimes complains that the Internet is a lawless land and that the same laws and rights that apply offline should apply online as well. In this, the Pirate Party could not agree more.

But unfortunately, what is happening is the opposite. Corporations are trying to take control over our communications tools, citing copyright concerns. Frequently, they are assisted by politicians who are also aspiring for the same control, citing terrorist concerns or some other McCarthyist scare word of the day. We should see this in perspective of the revolts that happened in 2011 in the Arab world.

There is a blind trust in authority here that is alarming. The ever-increasing desire to know what we talk about and to whom, and that desire is displayed openly by corporations and politicians alike, is a cause for much concern. To make matters worse, it is not just a matter of eavesdropping. Corporations and politicians openly want – and get – the right to silence us.

The copyright industry is demanding the right to kill switches to our very communications. If we talk about matters disruptive enough, disruptive according to authorities or according to the copyright industry, the line goes silent. Just twenty years ago, this would have been an absolutely horrifying prospect. Today, it is reality. Don't believe it? Try talking about a link to The Pirate Bay on MSN or on Facebook and watch as silence comes through. The copyright industry is fighting for this to become more pervasive. So are some politicians with agendas of their own.

While the copyright industry and repressive Big Brother politicians may not share the same ultimate motives, they are still pushing for exactly the same changes to society and control over our communications.

At the same time, citizens' physical movements are tracked to street level by the minute and the history recorded.

How would you revolt with all this in place, when all you said just fell silent before reaching the ears of others, and the regime could remotely monitor who met whom and where, and when they could kill all your equipment with the push of a button?

The West hardly has any high moral ground from where to criticize China or the regimes that are falling in the Arab world.

And yet, in all this darkness, there is a counter-reaction that is growing stronger by the day.

Activists are working through the night in defeating the surveillance and monitoring to ensure free speech by developing new tools in a cat-and-mouse game. These are the heroes of our generation. By ensuring free speech and free press, they are ensuring unmonitored, unblockable communications. Therefore, they are also defeating the copyright monopoly at its core, perhaps merely as a by-product.

Free and open software is at the core of the counter-reaction to Big Brother. It is open to scrutiny, which makes it impossible to install secret kill switches and wiretapping in it, and it can spread like wildfire when necessary. Moreover, it renounces the copyright monopoly to the point where popular development methods are actively fighting the monopoly, again making the connection between copyright enforcement and repression. Free operating systems and communications software are at the heart of all our future freedom of speech, as well as for the freedom of speech for regime topplers today.

The software that is being built by these hero activists is a guarantee for our civil liberties. Software like Tor and FreeNet and I2P, like TextSecure and RedPhone. That criminals can evade wiretapping is a cheap price to pay for our rights: Tomorrow, we might be the ones who are considered criminals for subversion. These are tools used by the people revolting against corrupt regimes today. We should learn something from that.

At the same time and by necessity, this free software makes the copyright monopoly unenforceable, as it creates the untappable, anonymous communication needed to guarantee our civil liberties. Mike Masnick of Techdirt recently noted that "piracy and freedom look remarkably similar".

Perhaps Freenet's policy expresses it the most clearly:

"You cannot guarantee free speech and enforce the copyright monopoly. Therefore, any technology designed to guarantee freedom of speech must also prevent enforcement of the copyright monopoly."

The fights for basic freedom of speech and for defeat of the copyright monopoly are one and the same. Therefore, the revolutions will happen using tools that are not just outside the copyright monopoly, but actively defeat it. The revolution will not be properly licensed.

Internet Blocking And Censorship

"Child pornography is great," the speaker at the podium declared enthusiastically. *"It's great because politicians understand child pornography. By playing that card, we can get them to act, and start blocking sites. And once they have done that, we can get them to start blocking file sharing sites"*.

The venue was a seminar organized by the American Chamber of Commerce in Stockholm on May 27, 2007, under the title *"Sweden — A Safe Haven for Pirates?"*. The speaker was Johan Schlüter from the Danish Anti-Piracy Group, a lobby organization for the music and film industry associations, like IFPI and others.

We were three pirates in the audience: Christian Engström, Rick Falkvinge, and veteran Internet activist Oscar Swartz. Oscar wrote a column about the seminar in Computer Sweden just after it had happened. Rick blogged about it later, and so did Christian.

"One day we will have a giant filter that we develop in close cooperation with IFPI and MPA. We continuously monitor the child porn on the net, to show the politicians that filtering works. Child porn is an issue they understand," Johan Schlüter said with a grin, his whole being radiating pride and enthusiasm from the podium.

And seen from the perspective of IFPI and the rest of the copyright lobby, he of course had every reason to feel both proud and enthusiastic, after the success he had had with this strategy in Denmark.

Today, the file sharing site The Pirate Bay is blocked by all major Internet service providers in Denmark. The strategy explained by Mr. Schlüter worked like clockwork.

Start with child porn, which everybody agrees is revolting, and find some politicians who want to appear like they are doing something. Never mind that the blocking as such is ridiculously easy to circumvent in less than 10 seconds. The purpose at this stage is only to get the politicians and the general public to accept the principle that censorship in the form of "filters" is okay. Once that principle has been established, it is easy to extend it to other areas, such as illegal file sharing. And once censorship of the Internet has been accepted in principle, they can start looking at ways to make it more technically difficult to circumvent.

In Sweden, the copyright lobby tried exactly the same tactic a couple of months after the seminar where Johan Schlüter had been speaking. In July 2007, the Swedish police was planning to add The Pirate Bay to the Swedish list of alleged child pornography sites, that are blocked by most major Swedish ISPs.

The police made no attempt whatsoever to contact anybody from The Pirate Bay, which they of course should have done if they had actually found any links to illegal pictures of sexual child abuse. The plan was to just censor the site, and at the same time create a guilt-by-association link between file sharing and child porn.

In the Swedish case, the plan backfired when the updated censorship list was leaked before it was put into effect. After an uproar in the blogosphere, the Swedish police was eventually forced to back down from the claim that they had found illegal child abuse pictures, or had any other legal basis for censoring the file sharing site. Unlike in Denmark, The Pirate Bay is not censored in Sweden today.

But the copyright lobby never gives up. If they are unable to get what they want on the national level, they will try through the EU, and vice versa.

The big film and record companies want censorship of the net, and they are perfectly willing to cynically use child porn as an excuse to get it. All they needed was a politician who was prepared to do their bidding, without spending too much effort on checking facts, or reflecting on the wisdom of introducing censorship on the net.

Unfortunately they found one in the newly appointed Swedish EU commissioner Cecilia Malmström. In March 2010 she presented an EU directive to introduce filtering of the net, exactly along to the lines that Johan Schlüter was advocating in his speech at the seminar in 2007. As drafted by the Commission, the directive would have forced member states to introduce blocking of sites alleged to contain child pornography.

Thanks to a lot of hard work from members of the European Parliament from several different political groups in the Committee for Fundamental Rights LIBE, the Commission's attempt to force the member states to introduce mandatory blocking was averted. The European Parliament changed the directive to say that member states *may*, as opposed to *shall*, introduce Internet blocking, but if they do, they must make sure that the procedure follows at least some legal minimum standards, and that the person whose website blocked has a right to appeal.

Since the directive does not mandate Internet blocking on the EU level, but leaves it up to the member states, we can expect the copyright industry to intensify their efforts to introduce Internet blocking on the national level in the countries that don't already have such systems in place. Although their real goal is to get the authorities to block sites like The Pirate Bay, the copyright industry will continue to use the child porn card wherever they judge it is too early to start talking about the censorship they really want.

But increasingly, they are beginning to feel that they no longer have to hide their real intentions. In the US, as this is being written in January 2012, Congress is debating a twin pair of laws called SOPA, Stop Online Piracy Act, and PIPA, Protect IP Act.

The idea behind SOPA and PIPA is to give US authorities the possibility to close down access to any website, hosted in any country in the world, if rights holders accuse it of infringing copyright, or "enabling or facilitating" copyright infringements. Just providing a link that "enables of facilitates" infringements can be enough to have a website shut down, or to have US credit card companies block all payments to the owner of the site. The decision will be taken by a US court, without hearing the accused party. In order to avoid being held liable themselves, Internet service providers and social platforms will have to start policing their clients and shut them off at the mere suspicion that they are doing anything that rights holders might object to.

With SOPA and PIPA, the copyright lobby is no longer using the pretext of child abuse pictures. Both laws are quite explicitly devoted to blocking sites on the net to protect holders of intellectual property rights.

Similar measures for Internet blocking are being proposed in Europe as well. UK academic Monica Horten at Iptegrity.com writes in January 2012:

The European Commission could ask ISPs to block content, and ask payment providers to withhold money on demand from rights-holders, following a policy announcement released today. The much-awaited announcement sets out EU official policy on the Internet and e-commerce. It follows a review of the E-commerce directive by the Commission.

The E-commerce directive to date has been the protector of the open Internet, notably the mere conduit provision. The review sets out pivotal changes which threaten that protecting role of mere conduit. Notably, the Commission wants to introduce a pan-European notice and action scheme. This is based on other 'notice and takedown' schemes (such as the one in the American DMCA law) but with an important difference. The proposed EU scheme uses the word 'action' instead of 'takedown', where action could mean asking hosts to take down content, but also would seem to mean blocking of content by ISPs on request:

"The notice and action procedures are those followed by the intermediary internet providers for the purpose of combating illegal content upon receipt of notification. The intermediary may, for example, take down illegal content, block it, or request that it be voluntarily taken down by the persons who posted it online."

In addition, the Commission wants to bring payment providers into 'co-operation' schemes between ISPs and rights-holders. This would mean asking the likes of PayPal, Mastercard, and Visa to block payments to websites or content providers, at the request of rights-holders:

"Cooperation between stakeholders, in particular internet providers, rights-holders and payment services, in the European Union and the US, may also help to combat illegal content."

Both the notice and action, and the payment 'co-operation' schemes pre-empt another European Commission review – the IPR Enforcement directive (IPRED). The IPRED review will consider EU-wide policy for enforcing copyright on the Internet. It is not clear whether the payments 'co-operation' would be positioned within the e-commerce directive or IPRED, or both.

Both directives are under the remit of the French Commissioner Michel Barnier, who is understood to be close to President Sarkozy.

This is where the Internet blocking issue stands in January, 2012.

When Commissioner Cecilia Malmström introduced her proposal to block child abuse pictures in 2010, she insisted in public that this was about child abuse images only, and not the beginning of a slippery slope towards general Internet censorship. In a keynote speech at a conference on May 6, 2010, she said:

> "[T]he Commission's proposal is about child abuse images, no more no less. The Commission has absolutely no plans to propose blocking of other types of content – and I would personally very strongly oppose any such idea."

Unless Ms. Malmström was actively lying at the time, it appears that she had not been briefed about quite the full net blocking agenda by her colleagues at the Commission, when she was given the task of introducing Internet censorship in EU legislation. To block sites for alleged copyright violations has been the goal of the copyright lobby all the time.

Shutting People Off The Internet

"Three strikes and you're out" is an expression that originates in baseball, and which American politicians have turned into a legal principle. In the context of Internet policy, "three-strikes" means that anyone accused of illegal file sharing three times by the rights holders is shut off from the Internet. "Graduated response" is another piece of jargon that is sometimes used and means the same thing.

In France there is the Hadopi law, where Internet service providers are required to shut down the connection for Internet users after they have received two warnings that a copyright holder suspects them of file sharing. In the UK, the Digital Economy Act says essentially the same. Italy, not wanting to be outdone in this race to the bottom, has proposed a "one-strike" law, where a single accusation of copyright infringement would be enough to have anyone banned from the Internet.

In essence, these laws leave it to the major film and record companies to act as judge and jury and point out individuals that they suspect of of file sharing, and then force the Internet service providers to execute the punishment by unplugging the connection.

Leaving aside for the moment the question of whether it is a good idea to let private companies take over the job of the legal system, how reasonable is shutting people off the Internet in the first place?

Let's consider what being disconnected actually means:

- *A ban on studying.* Most forms of education, in particular higher education, take Internet connectivity for granted. If you are a student, you will need Internet access for everything from practical things like finding out the schedule or turning in reports, to finding facts about the subject matter you are studying. Studies show that a majority of all students are file sharing. Should we cut off a majority of all students from their courses, or should we settle for making an example out of maybe 5-10% of them? What do the film and record companies think is a reasonable sacrifice to make?

- *A ban on running a business.* If you own a company, you are entirely dependent on the Internet today, no matter what line of business you're in. Contacting customers, updating your homepage, ordering supplies, answering e-mail – maybe you're selling goods via the Internet. Is it reasonable that the family business will go bankrupt because the fourteen-year old daughter in the family downloaded some pop music? Cutting off the Internet connection does not only punish the guilty party, but everyone in the household.

- *A ban on talking to friends.* Especially younger people keep in touch via the net. It's not strange or unusual to have best friends that you have never met, that you only socialize with using the Internet. This was not the case when most politicians were young, but the world has changed. To suddenly be thrown into solitary confinement is a very intrusive punishment, normally reserved for the most hardened and dangerous of criminals in prison.

- *Loss of citizen's rights.* If you wish to partake in public debate, you need access to the Internet today. Not only to keep up with the current issues, but also to be able to make your voice heard, be it via your own blog, commenting on others', Tweeting, organizing or joining Facebook groups and events.

"If you children are naughty, we'll take your toy away from you," is in effect what the politicians making these laws are saying to their citizens. But citizens are not children, and have no reason to listen to that kind of arrogant attitude from their elected representatives.

And the Internet is not a toy. It is an important part of society, and a piece of infrastructure that everyone needs access to in order to function in today's world. Politicians who fail to acknowledge this should not be surprised if the younger generation of voters finds them irrelevant.

Proportionality

In 2007, single US mother Jammie Thomas became a global file sharing martyr after she had been sued by a record company for 3.6 million dollars in damages. Her alleged crime was to have shared 24 songs on Kazaa (which used to be one of the most popular early file sharing services in the beginning of the '00s). The court convicted her, but reduced the damages to $222,000. In Ms. Thomas' case, that still amounted to more than five times her yearly income.

In the almost five years that have passed since the original verdict, the case has been appealed and re-appealed, and is still ongoing in January 2012. The damages have been going up and down in the various trials, from a whopping $1,920,000 in a re-trial in 2009, to $54,000 after a decision by a judge in 2011. The record company has declared that is not satisfied with this decision, and that it will be seeking to have the damages raised again.

But whether it's $2,000,000 or "merely" $50,000, this is clearly disproportionate for file sharing 24 songs. No matter how many songs you or your family members may have listened to without paying, you should not even have to think about the risk that you might be forced to sell your house or your car, or continue paying damages to record company for the rest of your life. That simply isn't proportionate.

In this case, it is not the money that the record company is after. They know Ms. Thomas doesn't have any, and yet they are said to have spent $3,000,000 on litigating the case so far. They want to set an example, to scare the general public into submission.

In the offline world, there is a long established principle of proportionality, which is one of the cornerstones of a just legal system. But the big rights holders have managed to persuade the legal system that this principle should not be applied to petty crimes and misdemeanors occurring online.

When it comes to copyright enforcement on the Internet, justice is blind – with rage. And unfortunately, this applies not only to US courts, but to European ones as well.

In Sweden in 2011, courts started handing out prison sentences to ordinary file sharers that had been unlucky enough to get caught by the rights holders' organizations. So far, it has only been a handful of cases, and in each of them the victim of the prosecution got the sentence suspended (since, being ordinary citizens picked more or less at random, none of them had a previous criminal record). But even so, from a legal point of view, the courts found that they had committed a crime that was grave enough to merit prison.

Is this really what we want in our society? There was a time when you could be sure that the headline "Sentenced to prison for listening to music illegally" would refer to a country like Cuba, the Soviet Union, or Chile under general Pinochet. Totalitarian regimes have always had the habit of putting people in prison for listening to music illegally, in order to protect the state against unwanted political influences.

But now we are seeing that headline being used to report court cases in what ought to be respectable EU member states, like Sweden. The purpose this time is not to protect the state against dangerous political thoughts, but to protect the entertainment industry against having to adapt to technological progress. But the sentences are the same: Prison for illegal music listening. Do we really think that this is proportionate, and represents the right way forward?

In 2008, a Danish man was sentenced to pay 160,000 Danish kroner (21,000 euro) for allegedly having shared 13,000 songs on a Direct Connect network in 2005. The verdict was later reduced by the Danish Supreme court in 2011, after 6 years of legal battles, but the first two courts that handled the case both thought that 20,000 euro was a perfectly reasonable punishment for an ordinary file sharer that happened to get picked as a scapegoat by the entertainment industry lawyers.

To put this in perspective, 13,000 songs is not very much by today's standards. 30 years ago, you would have needed a whole room full of LP records to have 13,000 songs, but today they will easily fit on a 64 GB USB stick in your pocket, which can be copied in minutes. Technology has changed the way that people think about and handle recorded music, especially for the younger generation. It is probably hard to find a Danish teenager who has not downloaded or shared a lot more than that.

Does this make it reasonable that all Danish families with teenagers should live under the threat of having to fork up 20,000 euro if an entertainment industry lawyer comes knocking at the door? Is listening to pop music illegally really as bad as stealing a 20,000 euro car and destroying it?

Today, courts in Europe haves a lot of discretion when deciding how much convicted file sharers have to pay in damages. This is why the Supreme Court could reduce the damages in the Danish case. But this may change if the European Parliament gives its consent to ratifying the controversial Anti-Counterfeiting Trade Agreement, ACTA.

Although the name of this treaty suggests that ACTA would be about commercial goods counterfeiting (which everybody, even the Pirate Party, agrees is a bad thing that should continue to be illegal), the implications of ACTA are much wider than that. In particular, ACTA aims to sharpen the enforcement of copyright on the Internet, in an attempt at combating file sharing.

According to ACTA, the damages for illegal file sharing will be higher, in some cases absurdly high.

In Article 9.1 of the ACTA agreement, it says that

> ... *In determining the **amount of damages** for infringement of intellectual property rights, a [signing country's] judicial authorities shall have the authority to consider, inter alia, any legitimate measure of value the right holder submits, which may include lost profits, the value of the infringed goods or services **measured by** the market price, or **the suggested retail price.***

(emphasis added)

In other words: To calculate the damages for having a disk full of illegally copied songs, you would multiply the number of songs with the suggested retail price for a song. But although this may look pretty harmless at first glance, it will lead to very drastic consequences in practice.

A two-terabyte disk can hold roughly half a million songs. If you calculate that at the market price of 1 euro per song, the damages for having a 2 TB disk full of music would be half a million euro.

Would that be proportionate or not? Remember that this is not an extreme example, it is something that lots of teenagers do. Would it really be proportionate that the family would have to sell their house and all their possessions if they were found out?

Under current European laws, damages are (at least in principle) limited to actual losses that the party that wins can show that he has actually suffered. They have to be proportional. Not even the lawyers for a film or record company would be able to convince a European court that they have actually lost half a million euro in non-purchases from a teenager who has never seen that kind of money in his life.

But according to ACTA, the film or record companies would no longer have to prove that they have actually lost the money. All they need to do is to multiply the number of songs with the price for one song to get the amount of damages measured by the suggested retail price.

A half million euro claim against a teenager with a 2 TB disk would be considered disproportionate and absurd by any European court today. With ACTA, awarding those damages becomes mandatory.

The copyright lobby knows this, or course. They have been deeply involved in the ACTA negotiations since day one. It is only the citizens and the elected members of parliaments that have been kept in the dark for as long as possible. The plan was to get ACTA signed, sealed, and delivered before too many elected politicians in parliaments knew the real consequences of ACTA as well.

We must now make sure that that plan does not work.

Due Process
In Sweden, with nine million inhabitants, about ten people get struck by lightning every year, and one or two of them die. This is of course very tragic, but this one-in-a-million risk is not enough to make people think that they themselves will get struck by lightning, and it is not enough to make them modify their behavior in any significant way. You will not see anybody wearing a protective hat with a lightning conductor if you walk down the streets of Stockholm.

Before 2011, the risk of getting convicted of illegal file sharing was about as high as the risk of getting killed by lightning. It happened at most to one or two people per year, so it was not something that anybody would seriously expect to happen to themselves.

In 2011, with three special prosecutors and ten police investigators focusing on file sharing crimes, the number of convictions went up to 8. Put in another way, this rather massive deployment of scarce judicial resources (which could otherwise have been spent on other crimes) only managed to get the risk of getting convicted for file sharing up to the risk of getting struck by lightning, as opposed to getting struck and killed. This is a considerable increase, but it is not enough to make file sharers modify their behavior in any significant way. Some may take the (sensible) precaution of spending five euros per month for an anonymizing service to hide their IP number, but a potential risk at the same level as the risk of getting struck by lightning will not make anybody stop sharing files.

To put the number of convictions in perspective, Swedish news agency TT reported that about 20% of the Swedish population, or 1.4 million people, are file sharing according to national statistics. About one third of them, or about half a million Swedes, are estimated to do it at a level that would render them prison sentences if they were found out. But of course, the vast majority of them never will be.

"We would need thousands of prosecutors" one of the three special file sharing prosecutors told the news agency, in full knowledge that this will never happen.

From the big film and record companies' perspective, using the courts to provide deterrence simply doesn't work. Deterrence has no effect unless the risk of getting caught is larger than microscopic. It isn't today. The judicial system does not have the capacity to bring entire generations to court at the same time. Cases going through the system are burdened with way too much debris like "evidence", "due process", and other red tape to create the volumes that the film and record companies need to ascertain effective deterrence. Unfortunately, they have realized this.

Therefore, they wish to make this whole process more efficient. In the US, their wishes have largely come true. The reason that the Jammie Thomas case got media attention wasn't that it was the first, or that the claims made by the record company were unusually outrageous. Those were exactly the same claims that the record companies had already made in thousands of similar cases. The Jammie Thomas case got attention because she was the first defendant that pleaded not guilty, and stood up to the music and film industry associations. Instead of folding and paying the offered settlement, she took this case to court.

Let's recap the numbers: The record company sued Thomas for $3.6 million, but offered a settlement out of court for $2,000. It is not difficult to understand why most people simply pay up, even if they are innocent. The mere threat of a costly court case and the risk of losing millions outweigh the relatively minor cost of a settlement. It's often smarter to just pay the blackmailer and move on.

Yes, blackmail. Organized blackmail. That is what this is all about. US record companies has sued 80-year old grandmothers, people with no computers and, in a few cases, long-dead people. By forcing ISPs to giving up customer records, these mass-mailed threats have evolved to a large industry in itself. There's no reason to be particular about who receives the threats, just send them out and wait for the protection money to roll in. There is no incentive to make sure that the defendants are actually guilty of anything, since the record companies never stand to lose anything.

The key to this strategy for the rights holders is that they can force the Internet service providers to disclose the name of the customer behind a certain IP number that is used on the Internet. If they have this, they can turn copyright enforcement from a cost to a profit center in its own right. Since only a small fraction of citizens who get a threatening legal letter are prepared to take the risk, and have the resources, to oppose it in court, the limited number of cases that the court system can process per year is not a problem for the scheme to work. To the rights holders, it's free money in exchange for a postage stamp.

The extent of this practice in Europe varies between the member states. In 2010, Danish film maker Lars von Trier made more money from threatening to sue people for allegedly downloading his film "Antichrist" illegally, than he got from box office returns and video and DVD sales combined. The business idea was completely straight-forward. All he had to do was to send out letters saying "pay us 1,200 euro immediately, or we'll sue you for five times that amount". Over 600 German recipients of the letter were sufficiently scared by the threat of a costly legal process to pay up. Even if some of them were in fact innocent, or if they just felt that 1,200 euro was a pretty unreasonable punishment for having watched a movie (that wasn't even particularly successful at the box office) for free, they decided it was not worth the risk to have their day in court.

Sweden, on the other hand, has so far mostly been spared this type of behavior by the rights holders. This is because we used to have laws that prevented the Internet service providers from disclosing information about which of its customers had a certain IP number at a certain time, according to Swedish data protection laws. Instead, the film and record companies have had to file a criminal complaint and let the police investigate if a crime has been committed. This is not enough for the rights holders, since the criminal justice system does not have the capacity to get the volumes up to the level that the rights holders want.

This may change, however, now that Sweden has implemented the Intellectual Property Rights Enforcement Directive "IPRED", and is working to implement the Data Retention Directive as well. These two directives were designed from the outset to work in tandem, in order to give rights holders the practical means to implement the strategy of legal threats.

The Data Retention Directive forces the Internet service providers to keep logs that connect an IP number to one of their customers, and the Ipred directive is intended to ensure that the rights holders and their anti-piracy organizations can demand to get access to the information. If implemented the way the rights holders want them to be, these two directives together open up the door for US-style legalized blackmail of ordinary citizens.

The fundamental problem is that if laws have the effect of enabling private companies to set up their own enforcement system where the vast majority of cases are handled outside the courts, citizens can no longer expect due process to be observed. The important thing is not what might happen in the court of last instance, but the cost of getting there. If you as a citizen cannot afford to take the risk of having your case tried in a proper manner, you are being denied justice in practice.

...And It Isn't Working Anyway

In June 2010, I (Christian Engström) attended a working group meeting on copyright enforcement in the European Parliament. As guests, we had representatives from the Motion Picture Association MPA, and from the record producers' organization IFPI. These two organizations represent the hard core of the copyright lobby.

The representative from IFPI talked about how many fantastic things the record companies would put on the market, if only online piracy could be eliminated or reduced. To achieve this, she was asking for information campaigns aimed at Internet users, and stricter sanctions against copyright infringers.

She showed a slide with the words

"The music industry favours an approach which combines the information of Internet users, with sanctions for persistent infringers."

This is exactly what the copyright industry always says, and has been saying for over a decade. Information campaigns about copyright directed at Internet users, and sanctions handed out by the Internet service provider companies, preferably without any involvement of courts.

But leaving all other aspects aside, do we have any reason to think that this will be effective?

When it was my turn to ask a question, I reminded IFPI and the MPA that they have more than a decade's experience of this strategy, in both the US and Europe. It was in 1998 that DMCA, the Digital Millennium Copyright Act, was adopted in the US. In Europe we have seen a number new laws for stricter enforcement being introduced over the years, notably the 2001 Copyright Directive EUCD, and the 2004 Intellectual Property Rights Enforcement Directive IPRED. We have also seen a number of information campaigns, often saying that "file sharing is theft".

With so much experience from a number of countries, the rights holder's organizations are of course in a very good position to judge how effective the strategy has been.

"Could you tell us about these experiences, and could you give any examples where illegal file sharing in a country had been eliminated or greatly reduced by information campaigns and sanctions?" I asked the representatives from IFPI and the MPA.

The representative from IFPI said that so far, the strategy had not been very successful. This was because the rights holders are forced to go through the courts to punish illegal file sharers, which severely restricts the number of cases they are able to pursue.

IFPI and the other rights holders would need to make a more wide-scale mass response in order to create an effective deterrent, she said. She was hoping that the EU would come to the rescue with legislation to allow this.

When it came to giving an example of a country where stricter enforcement had led to significantly reduced file sharing, she mentioned Sweden, where the IPRED directive was implemented on April 1, 2009.

So let's look at the graph for the total Internet traffic in Sweden around that time:

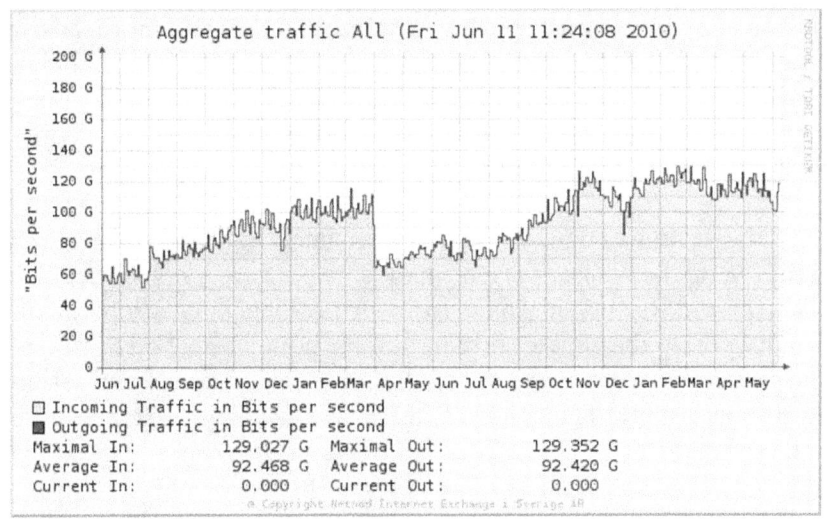

Aggregate traffic All (Fri Jun 11 11:24:08 2010)

```
200 G
180 G
160 G
140 G
120 G
100 G
 80 G
 60 G
 40 G
 20 G
    0
     Jun Jul Aug Sep Oct Nov Dec Jan FebMar Apr May Jun Jul Aug Sep Oct Nov Dec Jan FebMar Apr May
```

"Bits per second"

☐ Incoming Traffic in Bits per second
■ Outgoing Traffic in Bits per second

Maximal In:	129.027 G	Maximal Out:	129.352 G
Average In:	92.468 G	Average Out:	92.420 G
Current In:	0.000	Current Out:	0.000

@ Copyright Netnod Internet Exchange i Sverige AB

Internet traffic in Sweden, two-year graph by Netnod

It is indeed true that there was a sharp drop in the total network traffic, by about 40 per cent, on the day the Ipred law came into force in Sweden. IFPI and the other anti-piracy organizations immediately sent out jubilant press releases saying that the Ipred law really worked. This has been the line that they have maintained ever since.

But when we look at the graph, we see that six months later, the network traffic was back to where it used to be. If this was a success for the sanctions strategy against file sharing, it was a very short-lived one.

And this is how it has been all over the world. Just like IFPI told the working group in the European Parliament, information to Internet users and stricter sanctions have so far been unable to stem the tide of illegal file sharing. But they still hope that more of the same will be effective.

There is nothing to suggest that their hopes have any base in reality. The "information and enforcement" strategy simply isn't working, no matter how much they or anybody else would want it to.

The copyright industry just wants more, more, and more, and it doesn't think twice about ruining our hard-won fundamental civil liberties to prop up their crumbling monopoly and control. When one tough measure doesn't work — and they never do — the copyright industry keeps demanding more.

A few centuries ago, the penalty for unauthorized copying was breaking on the wheel. It is a term most people are not very familiar with these days, but it was a form of prolonged torturous death penalty where the convict first had every bone in his body broken, and then was weaved into the spokes of a wagon wheel and set up on public display. The cause of death was usually thirst, a couple of days later.

The copy monopoly in those days concerned fabric patterns. It was in 18th century France, prior to the revolution. Some patterns were more popular than others, and to get some additional revenue to the Crown's tax coffers, the King sold a monopoly on these patterns to selected members of the nobility, who in turn could charge an arm and a leg for them (and did so).

But the peasants and commoners could produce these patterns themselves. They could produce pirated copies of the fabrics, outside of the nobility's monopoly. So the nobility went to the King and demanded that the monopoly they had bought with good money should be upheld by the King's force.

The King responded by introducing penalties for pirating these fabrics. Light punishments at first, then gradually tougher. Towards the end, the penalty was death by public torture, drawn out over several days. And it wasn't just a few poor sods who were made into public examples.

Swedish economist and historian Eli Heckscher writes in his standard work *Merkantilismen*:

Of course, the attempt to stop a development supported by a violent fashion trend, carried by the [...] influential female kin, could impossibly succeed. The policy is considered to have cost 16,000 people their lives, through executions and armed clashes, plus the yet uncounted who were sentenced to slavery on galleys and other punishments. In Valence, on one single occasion, 77 people were sentenced to hang, 58 to be broken on the wheel and 631 to the galleys, one was acquitted, and none were pardoned. But this was so far from effective, that the use of printed calico spread through all social groups during this period, in France and elsewhere.

Sixteen thousand people, almost exclusively common folks, died by execution or in the violent clashes that surrounded the monopoly.

Here's the fascinating part:

Capital punishment didn't even make a dent in the pirating of the fabrics. Despite the fact that most people knew somebody personally who had been executed by public torture, the copying continued unabated at the same level.

So the question that needs asking is this:

For how long will the politicians continue to listen to the copyright industry's demands for harsher punishments for copying, when we learn from history that no punishment that mankind is capable of inventing has the ability to deter people from sharing and copying things they like?

To get the issue of illegal file sharing off the table, we must find another solution. But that is no problem, because such a solution exists.

Once you accept that copyright must be scaled back, a whole palette of advantages to that scenario become apparent. Two billion human beings would have 24/7 access to all of humanity's collective knowledge and culture. That's a much larger leap for civilization than when public libraries arrived in 1850. No public cost or new tax is involved. All the infrastructure is already in place. The technology has been developed, and the tools are deployed. All we have to do is lift the ban on using them.

File Sharing And Fundamental Rights – The Bottom Line

The relationship between file sharing and fundamental rights is very simple:

• *File sharing is here to stay.* No matter what the Pirate Party or anybody else will or won't do, it is not going to change this fact. In the long run, it will become impossible to charge money for just digital copies. This is a piece of technological history, and there is nothing more to discuss.

• *So why bother?* The copyright industry will not be able to stop file sharing. The file sharers will find ways of protecting themselves through anonymization, encryption, etc, as needed. No problems for them. But the copyright industry will try to set examples by punishing random individuals in a hard and disproportionate way.

This is not acceptable. An even bigger problem is the general surveillance of everybody's private communication, and the censorship and blocking systems that the copyright industry is proposing. For this reason, we must take the political fight to align copyright legislation with reality.

This is really all there is to it. The only way to even try to reduce file sharing is to introduce mass surveillance of all Internet users. Even this is not very effective, as experiences from the last decade have shown. But if you want to fight file sharing, mass surveillance is the only way. The copyright industry knows this.

So, even those who do think that file sharing is harmful to society and should be eradicated, have to ask the question if they are prepared to accept the surveillance society to achieve this. Because once the surveillance systems have been installed, they can be used for any purpose that the ones in charge of them see fit.

You may well feel that you have "nothing to hide" right now when it comes to file sharing, if you are not doing it. But can you be certain that you will always have "nothing to hide" when it comes to expressing views that future governments may not like? How do you know that you would want to be unquestioningly loyal to the government the next time it slips into McCarthyism, or worse, and starts listing and blacklisting people with certain political sympathies?

If you build a system for mass surveillance, there will be a system for mass surveillance ready the day someone wants to use it for other purposes. This is the bottom line in the file sharing debate.

Chapter 4

Copyright Is Not Property

The Copyright Monopoly
Is A Limitation Of Property Rights

The concept of property is older than history, probably as old as mankind itself.

But the copyright monopoly is not a property right. It is a limitation of property rights. Copyright is a government-sanctioned private monopoly that limits what people may do with things they have legitimately bought.

All too often, we hear the copyright lobby talk about theft, about property, about how they are robbed of something when someone makes a copy. This is, well, factually incorrect. It is a use of words that are carefully chosen to communicate that the copyright monopoly is property, or at the very least comparable to property rights.

This is only rhetoric from the copyright lobby in an attempt to justify the monopoly as righteous: to associate "the copyright monopoly" with a positive word such as "property". However, when we look at the monopoly in reality, it is a limitation of property rights.

Let's compare two pieces of property: a chair and a DVD.

When I buy a chair, I hand over money for which I get the chair and a receipt. This chair has been mass-produced from a master copy at some sort of plant. After the money has changed hands, this particular chair is mine. There are many more like it, but this one is mine. I have bought one of many identical copies and the receipt proves it.

As this copy of the chair is mine, exclusively mine, there are a number of things I can do with it. I can take it apart and use the pieces for new hobby projects, which I may choose to sell, give away, put out as exhibits or throw away. I can put it out on the porch and charge neighbors for using it. I can examine its construction, produce new chairs from my deductions with some raw material that is also my property, and do whatever I like with the new chairs, particularly including selling them.

All of this is normal for property. It is mine; I may do what I like with it. Build copies, sell, display, whatever.

As a sidetrack, this assumes that there are no patents on the chair. However, assuming that the invention of the chair is older than 20 years, any filed patents on this particular invention have expired. Therefore, patents are not relevant for this discussion.

Now, let's jump to what happens when I buy a movie.

When I buy a movie, I hand over money and I get the DVD and a receipt. This movie has been mass-produced from a master copy at some sort of plant. After the money has changed hands, this particular movie is mine. There are many more like it, but this one is mine. I have bought one of many identical copies and the receipt proves it.

But despite the fact that this copy of the movie is mine, exclusively mine, there are a number of things that I may not do with it, prohibited from doing so by the copyright monopoly held by somebody else. I may *not* use pieces of the movie for new hobby projects that I sell, give away, or put out as exhibits. I may *not* charge the neighbors for using it on the porch. I may *not* examine its construction and produce new copies. All of these rights would be normal for property, but the copyright monopoly is a severe limitation on my property rights for items I have legitimately bought.

It is not possible to say that I own the the DVD when viewed in one way but not when viewed in another. There is a clear definition of property, and the receipt says I own the DVD in *all* its interpretations and aspects. Every part of the shape making up the DVD is mine. The copyright monopoly, however, limits how I can use my own property.

This doesn't inherently mean that the copyright monopoly is bad. It does, however, mean that the monopoly cannot be defended from the standpoint that property rights are good. If you take your stand from there, you will come to the conclusion that the copyright monopoly is bad as it is a limitation of property rights.

Defending the copyright monopoly with the justification that property rights are sacred is quite like defending the death penalty for murder with the justification that life is sacred. There may be other, valid, justifications for defending the copyright monopoly and these limitations of property rights — but that particular chain of logic just doesn't hold.

But if copyright isn't a property right, what is it and where does it come from, and how did it become such a big thing in today's society? To answer these questions, we shall have a look at the history of copyright. It turns out that it differs quite strongly from what you usually hear from the copyright industry.

1400s: The Printing Press Threatens To Disrupt Power

We're starting with the advent of the Black Death in Western Europe in the 1350s. Like all other places, Europe was hit hard: people fled westward from the Byzantine Empire and brought with them both the plague and scientific writings. It would take Europe 150 years to recover politically, economically and socially.

The religious institutions were the ones to recover the slowest. Not only were they hit hard because of the dense congregation of monks and nuns, but they were also the last to be repopulated, as parents needed every available child in the family's economy, agriculture, etc, in the decades following the plague.

This is relevant because monks were the ones making books in this time. When you wanted a book copied, you would go to a scribe at a monastery, and they would copy it for you. By hand. No copy would be perfect; every scribe would fix spelling and grammatical errors while making the copy, as well as introduce some new ones.

Also, since all scribes were employed (read controlled) by the Catholic Church, there was quite some limitation to what books would be produced. Not only was the monetary cost of a single book astronomical — one copy of The Bible required 170 calfskins or 300 sheepskins (!!) — but there was also a limit to what teachings would be reproduced by a person of the clergy. Nothing contradicting the Vatican was even remotely conceivable.

By 1450, the monasteries were still not repopulated, and the major cost of having a book copied was the services of the scribe, an undersupplied craft still in high demand. This puts things in proportion, given the astronomical cost of the raw materials and that they were a minor cost in ordering a book. In 1451, Gutenberg perfected the combination of the squeeze press, metal movable type, oil based print inks and block printing. At the same time, a new type of paper had been copied from the Chinese, a paper which was cheap to make and plentiful. This made scribecraft obsolete more or less overnight.

The printing press revolutionized society by creating the ability to spread information cheaply, quickly and accurately.

The Catholic Church, which had previously controlled all information (and particularly held a cornered market on the scarcity of information), went on a rampage. They could no longer control what information would be reproduced, could no longer control what people knew, and lobbied kings across Europe for a ban on this technology which wrestled control of the populace from them.

Many arguments were used to justify this effort, trying to win the hearts of the people for going back to the old order. One notable argument was "How will the monks get paid?".

The Catholic Church would eventually fail in this endeavor, paving the way for the Renaissance and the Protestant movement, but not before much blood had been spilled in trying to prevent the accurate, cheap and quick distribution of ideas, knowledge and culture.

This attempt culminated in France on January 13, 1535, when a law was enacted at the request of the Catholic Church, a law which forced the closure of all bookshops and stipulated death penalty by hanging for anybody using a printing press.

This law was utterly ineffective. Pirate print shops lined the country's borders like a pearl necklace and pirate literature poured into France through contraband distribution channels built by ordinary people hungry for more things to read.

1500s: Bloody Mary Invents Copyright

On May 23, 1533, the 17 year old girl who would later become Mary I of England was formally declared a bastard by the archbishop. Her mother, Catherine, who was a Catholic and the Pope's protégé, had been thrown out of the family by her father Henry, who had converted to Protestantism just to get rid of Catherine. This was an injustice Mary would attempt to correct all her life.

King Henry VIII wanted a son to inherit the Throne of England for the Tudor dynasty, but his marriage was a disappointment. His wife, Catherine of Aragon, had only borne him a daughter, Mary. Worse still, the Pope would not let him divorce Catherine in the hope of finding someone else to bear him a son.

Henry's solution was quite drastic, effective and novel. He converted all of England into Protestantism, founding the Church of

England, in order to deny the Pope any influence over his marriage. Henry then had his marriage with Catherine of Aragon declared void on May 23, 1533, after which he went on to marry several other women in sequence. He had a second daughter with his second wife, and finally a son with his third wife. Unlike the bastard child Mary, her younger half-siblings — Elizabeth and Edward — were Protestants.

Edward succeeded Henry VIII to the throne in 1547, at the age of nine. He died before reaching adult age. Mary was next in the line of succession, despite having been declared a bastard. Thus, the outcast ascended to the Throne of England with a vengeance as Mary I in 1553.

She had not spoken to her father for years and years. Rather, hers was the mission to undo her father's wrongdoings to the Faith, to England, and to her mother, and to return England to Catholicism. She persecuted Protestants relentlessly, publicly executing several hundred, and earning herself the nickname *Bloody Mary*.

She shared the concern of the Catholic Church over the printing press. The public's ability to quickly distribute information *en masse* was dangerous for her ambitions to restore Catholicism, in particular their ability to distribute heretic material. (Political material, in this day and age, was not distinguishable from religious material.) Seeing how France had failed miserably in banning the printing press, even under threat of hanging, she realized another solution was needed. One that involved the printing industry in a way that would benefit them as well.

She devised a monopoly where the London printing guild would get a complete monopoly on all printing in England, in exchange for her censors determining what was fit to print beforehand. It was a very lucrative monopoly for the guild, who would be working hard to maintain the monopoly and the favor of the Queen's censors. This merger of corporate and governmental powers turned out to be effective in suppressing free speech and political-religious dissent.

The monopoly was awarded to the London Company of Stationers on May 4, 1557. It was called *copyright*.

It was widely successful as a censorship instrument. Working with the industry to suppress free speech worked, in contrast to the French attempt in the earlier 1500s to ban all printing by decree. The Stationers worked as a private censorship bureau, burning unlicensed books, impounding or destroying monopoly-infringing printing presses, and denying politically unsuitable material from seeing the light of day. Only in doubtful cases did they care to consult the Queen's censors for advice on what was allowed and what was not. Mostly, it was quite apparent after a few initial consultations.

There was obviously a lust for reading, and the monopoly was very lucrative for the Stationers. As long as nothing politically destabilizing was in circulation, the common people were allowed their entertainment. It was a win-win for the repressive Queen and for the Stationers with a lucrative monopoly on their hands.

Mary I died just one year later, on November 17, 1558. She was succeeded by her Protestant half-sister Elizabeth, who went on to become Elizabeth I and one of the highest-regarded regents of England ever. Mary's attempts to restore Catholicism to England had failed. Her invention of copyright, however, survives to this day.

1600s – 1700s: The Monopoly Dies And Is Resurrected

After Bloody Mary had enacted the copyright censorship monopoly in 1557, neither the profitable industry guild nor the censoring Crown had any desire to abolish it. It would stand for 138 years uninterrupted.

As we have seen, the copyright monopoly was instituted as a censorship mechanism by Mary I in 1557 to prevent people from discussing or disseminating Protestant material. Her successor, Elizabeth I, was just as happy to keep the monopoly after Mary's death in 1558 to prevent people from discussing or disseminating *Catholic* material.

During the 1600s, Parliament gradually tried to wrestle control of the censorship from the Crown. In 1641, Parliament abolished the court where copyright cases had been tried, the infamous Star Chamber. In effect, this turned violation of the monopoly into a sentence-less crime, much like jaywalking in Sweden today: While it was still technically a crime, and technically illegal, you could not be tried for it and there was no punishment. As a result, creativity in Britain soared.

Unfortunately, this wasn't what Parliament had had in mind at all.

In 1643, the copyright censorship monopoly was reinstituted with a vengeance. It included demands for pre-registrations of author, printer and publisher with the London Company of Stationers, a requirement for publication license before publishing anything, the right for the Stationers to impound, burn and destroy unlicensed equipment and books, and arrests and harsh punishments for anybody violating the copyright censorship.

Fast-forwarding a bit, there was something called the Glorious Revolution in 1688, and Parliament's composition changed radically to mostly people who had previously been at the business end of censorship and weren't all too keen for that to continue. Therefore, the Stationers' monopoly was made to expire in 1695.

So from 1695 onward, there was no copyright. None. Creativity soared – again – and historians claim that many of the documents that eventually led to the founding of the United States of America were written in this time.

Unfortunately, the London Company of Stationers were not happy at all with the new order where they had lost their lucrative monopoly. They gathered their families on the stairs of Parliament and begged for the monopoly to be reinstated.

It is noteworthy that authors did not ask for the copyright monopoly, the printers and distributors did. There was never an argument along the lines that nothing would be written without copyright. The argument was that nothing would be printed without copyright. This is something else entirely.

Parliament, having just abolished censorship, was keen on not reinstituting a central point of control with a possible abuse potential. The Stationers responded by suggesting that writers should "own" their works. In doing so, they killed three birds with one stone. One, Parliament would be assured that there was no central point of control which could be used to censor. Two, the publishers would retain a monopoly for all intents and purposes, as the writers would have nobody to sell their works to but the publishing industry. Three, and perhaps most importantly, the monopoly would be legally classified as Anglo-Saxon Common Law rather than the weaker Case Law, and therefore given much stronger legal protection.

They publishing lobby got as they wanted, and the new copyright monopoly was re-enacted in 1709, taking effect on April 10, 1710. This was the copyright lobby's first major victory.

What we see at this point in history is copyright in its unspun form: a monopoly with heritage from censorship where artists and authors were not even considered, but where it was always for the publishers' profit.

Also, the Stationers would continue to impound, destroy and burn others' printing presses for a long time, despite not having the right any longer. Abuse of power came immediately, and would last until the pivotal Entick vs. Carrington case in 1765, when yet another of these raids for "unlicensed" (read unwanted) authors had taken place. In the verdict of this court case in 1765, it was firmly established that no right may be denied to any citizen if not expressly forbidden by law, and that no authority may take upon itself any right not explicitly given by law.

Thus, the very first foundations of modern democracy and civil liberties were won in the battle against the copyright monopoly. There is nothing new under the sun.

1800s: Reading Books Without Paying? That's Stealing!

When the United States was founded, the concept of monopolies on ideas was carried to the New World and debated intensely. Thomas Jefferson was a fierce opponent to the monster of monopolies on ideas. A compromise was reached.

Copyright didn't originate in the United States, as we have seen. The idea had been there beforehand and the Founding Fathers carried the laws with them into their new country. The topic of monopolies on ideas, however, was a topic not easily settled. Jefferson wrote:

If nature has made any one thing less susceptible than all others of exclusive property, it is the action of the thinking power called an idea, which an individual may exclusively possess as long as he keeps it to himself; but the moment it is divulged, it forces itself into the possession of every one, and the receiver cannot dispossess himself of it. Its peculiar character, too, is that no one possesses the less, because every other possesses the whole of it. He who receives an idea from me, receives instruction himself without lessening mine; as he who lights his taper at mine, receives light without darkening me. That ideas should freely spread from one to another over the globe, for the moral and mutual instruction of man, and improvement of his condition, seems to have been peculiarly and benevolently designed by nature, when she made them ... incapable of confinement or exclusive appropriation.

In the end, the United States Constitution was the first one to specify the reason for copyrights (and patents!) to be granted. It is very clear and straightforward in its justification for the existence of copyright in United States law:

...to promote the progress of the sciences and useful arts...

It is particularly notable that the purpose of the monopoly was not for any profession to make money, neither writer nor printer nor distributor. Instead, the purpose is exemplary in its clarity: the only justification for the monopoly is if it *maximizes the culture and knowledge available to society.*

Thus, copyright (in the US, and therefore predominantly today) is a balance between the public's access to culture and the same public's interest of having new culture created. This is tremendously important. In particular, note here that the public is the only legitimate stakeholder in the wording and evolution of copyright law. The monopoly holders, while certainly being beneficiaries of the monopoly, are not legitimate stakeholders and should have no say in its wording, just like a regiment town should have no say in whether that regiment is actually needed for national security.

It is useful to point at the wording of the US Constitution when people falsely believe that the copyright monopoly exists so that artists can make money. It never did, not in any country.

Meanwhile in the United Kingdom
In the meantime in the United Kingdom, books were still quite expensive, mostly because of the copyright monopoly. Book collections were only seen in rich men's homes, and some started benevolently to lend books to the common people.

The publishers went mad about this, and lobbied Parliament to outlaw the reading of a book without first paying for their own copy. They tried to outlaw the public library before the library had even been invented. *"Reading without paying first? That's stealing from the authors! Taking the bread right out of their children's mouths!"*

But Parliament took a different stance, seeing the positive impact of reading on society. The problem perceived by Parliament was not the self-described eternal plight of the copyright monopolists, but the problem that rich men in society dictated who would read and who wouldn't. It seemed beneficial to society to level the playing field: to create public libraries, accessible to poor and rich alike.

The copyright monopolists went absolutely ballistic when they heard about this idea. *"You can't let anybody read any book for free! Not a single book will be sold ever again! Nobody will be able to live off their writing! No author will write a single book ever again if you pass this law!"*

Parliament in the 1800s was much wiser than today, however, and saw the copyright monopolists' tantrum for what it was. Parliament took a strong stance that public access to knowledge and culture had a larger benefit to society than the copyright monopoly, and so in 1849, the law instituting public libraries in the UK was passed. The first public library opened in 1850.

And as we know, not a single book has been written ever since. Either that, or the copyright monopolists' rant about nothing being created without a strong monopoly was as false then as it is when repeated today.

(Note: in some European countries, authors and translators get some pennies for every book lent from a library. It should be strongly noted that this is not a compensation for an imaginary loss of income, as if every reduction in the monopoly required compensation, but a national cultural grant which happens to measure popularity and therefore suitability for that grant using statistics from libraries. Besides, the grant appeared in the early 1900s, long after libraries.)

Meanwhile in Germany

Germany had no copyright monopoly during this time. Several historians argue that this led to the rapid proliferation of knowledge that enabled Germany to take the industrial lead over the United Kingdom – knowledge could be spread cheaply and efficiently. So in a way, Germany's leapfrogging of the United Kingdom proved the British Parliament was right: The national interest of access to culture and knowledge does supersede the monopoly interest of the publishers.

Late 1800s: Moral Rights On The Continent

In the late 1800s, the publishers' ever-strengthening copyright monopoly had lopsided the creators' chances of making any revenue from their works. Basically, all the money went to publishers and distributors, and creators were left starving, due to the copyright monopoly. (Just like today.)

A person in France named *Victor Hugo* would take the initiative to try to level the playing field by internationalizing a French tradition known as *droit d'auteur*, "writer's right", into the copyright monopoly. Also, he would try to make the copyright monopoly international: until now, it had just been a national monopoly. A French writer could sell his monopoly to a French publisher, and the publisher would enjoy monopoly powers in France, but not in Germany or the United Kingdom. Hugo sought to change this.

Paradoxically, the copyright and patent monopolies were forgotten when free market laws were enacted across Europe in the mid-1800s. Patent law still talks about "prevention of disloyal competition" as justification for its existence, which is a remnant from when guilds dictated products, craftsmen, and prices. If a business practices *loyal competition* in their industry segment today, we raid them at dawn and haul their ass to court. The copyright monopoly is a similar remnant from the printing guild of London.

Victor Hugo would try to balance the immense powers of the publishers by giving creators some rights under the copyright monopoly as well, unfortunately impoverishing the public further. (It is important here to remember that there are three parties to the copyright conflict: creators, publishers, and the public. Ironically, the publishers, who are the party least necessary to sustain a culturally rich society, are the ones with the by far strongest position in the monopoly's design.)

While Hugo didn't live to see the fruition of his initiative, the *Berne Convention* was signed in 1886. It said that countries should respect the copyrights of other countries, and an agency — BIRPI — was set up as watchdog. This agency has mutated, grown and swelled and is today WIPO, which still oversees the Berne Convention, which has also swelled, mutated and been hijacked twice. (More on this in the next section.)

So, at this point, there are four aspects of the copyright monopoly, which have more differences between them than similarities:

1. The commercial monopoly to fixations of a work. This is the original monopoly granted to London's printing guild in exchange for censorship.

2. The commercial monopoly to performances of a work. If somebody performs a work publicly on a for-profit stage, the monopoly holder has a right to demand money.

3. The *droit moral* to be acknowledged as creator. The right for an author or artist to be acknowledged as creator of his or her work, acting as protection against counterfeiting and against plagiarism.

4. The *droit moral* to veto an improper performance of the work. If an artist feels that a performance slights the work or the name of the artist, they have the right to deny that performance the light of day.

The *droits morals* are very different in nature from the commercial monopolies in that they cannot be sold or transferred. This sets them sharply apart from the justification that convinced the British Parliament to re-enact the copyright monopoly in 1709.

It is also noteworthy how often these four aspects are deliberately confused to defend the most controversial and damaging of the monopolies, the commercial monopoly on fixations (and later duplication). You will often hear people from the copyright industry defending the monopoly by asking "would you want somebody else to take your work and claim it was theirs?". However, this is the quite uncontroversial third part, the *droit moral* of attribution and credit, which cannot honestly be used to defend any of the two commercial monopolies.

The United States didn't like moral rights, by the way, so they stayed outside of the Berne Convention until they could use it for leverage against Toyota a hundred years later. We'll return to that later.

1930s: Hijacked By The Record Industry

During most of the 20th century, a battle of prominence raged between performing musicians and the record industry. For most of the century, musicians were regarded as the important party in law and in common sense. However, the record industry would rather see music under corporate control. Active intervention by the self-declaredly fascist regime in Italy tipped the scales in this direction.

Copyright in the 20th century was not characterized by books, but by music. The 1930s saw two major developments that affected musicians: the Great Depression, which caused many musicians to lose their jobs, and movies with sound, which caused most of the rest of musicians to lose their jobs.

In this environment, two initiatives were taken in parallel. Musicians' unions tried to guarantee income and sustenance to the people who were now jobless. Unions all over the West were concerned about the spread of "mechanized music": any music that isn't performed live and therefore didn't need performing musicians. They wanted some power over the speaker technology, and the question was raised through the International Labour Organization (a predecessor to the UN agency with the same name).

At the same time, the record industry tried to exert the exact same power over speakers, radio and musicians. However, the entire political and business world at that time regarded them as a service contractor to the musicians. They could go about running their business if they were service-minded enough, or go bankrupt trying, and weren't worth diddlysquat more than that to anyone. Anyone, with just one exception:

Fascist Italy.

(This word, *fascist*, is loaded with emotion today. Italy's regime at this time were *self-declared* fascists. We are using the word to describe them exactly as they described themselves.)

In 1933, the phonographic industry was invited to Rome by the *Confederazione Generale Fascista dell'Industria Italiana* and under protection of the same. At this conference, held on November 10-14, an international federation of the phonographic industry was formed. It would later be better known under its acronym, IFPI. It was agreed that IFPI would try to work within the Berne Convention to establish producers' rights similar to those of the musicians and artists (which were always sold to publishers).

IFPI continued to meet in countries which welcomed their corporatist agenda, so they met in Italy the next year too, in Stresa. 1935 and onwards proved a bit turbulent for the world at large, but Italy still enacted corporatist rights of the record industry in 1937.

Negotiations for a copyright-like monopoly, attached to Berne and therefore international, was still too tempting for the record industry to resist. So after the war, IFPI reconvened in para-fascist Portugal in 1950. Italy wasn't suitable anymore, and the conference readied a draft text that would give them copyright-identical monopolies, so-called "neighboring rights", for producing and printing creative works such as music. This monopoly would be practically identical to the commercial copyright monopoly for fixations of a creative work.

The neighboring rights were ratified by BIRPI (today WIPO) in 1961 in the so-called Rome Convention, giving the record industry copyright-identical monopolies. At the same time, ILO's attempt to give musicians similar rights had flopped, waned, and failed.

Since 1961, the record industry has feverishly defended copyright, despite the fact that it doesn't enjoy any copyright monopoly, only the copyright-identical monopoly known as "neighboring rights".

One needs to remember two things at this point:

First, the record industry is confusing all these monopolies on purpose. It keeps defending "its copyright", which it doesn't have, and talks nostalgically about how this copyright monopoly was created in great wisdom during the dawn of the Enlightenment [insert sunset and kittens here], referring to the Statute of Anne in 1709, which wasn't the first copyright anyway. In reality, the neighboring-rights monopolies were created in Europe as late as 1961. These monopolies have been controversial and questioned from day one in 1961, and were certainly not the product of any Enlightenment wisdom.

Second, we were but a hair's breadth from still regarding record labels as service bureaus for musicians, had ILO not failed, instead of the stranglehold on musicians that they have been for the past decades. This would have been the case if it had not been for two intervening fascist governments – fascist in the literal sense of the word – supporting the record industry in corporatizing society and becoming the copyright industry.

1980s: Hijacked Again – By Pfizer

Toyota struck at the heart of the American soul in the 1970s, and all her politicians started carrying mental "The End Is Nigh" signs. The most American things of all – cars! The American Cars! – weren't good enough for the American people. They all bought Toyota instead. This was an apocalypse-grade sign that United States was approaching its end as an industrial nation, unable to compete with Asia.

This is the final part in my series about the history of the copyright monopoly. The period of 1960 to 2010 is marked by two things: one, the record-label-driven creepage of the copyright monopoly into the noncommercial, private domain where it was always a commercial-only monopoly before ("home taping is illegal" and such nonsense) and the monopoly therefore threatening fundamental human rights, and two, the corporate political expansion of the copyright monopoly and other monopolies. As most people are aware of the former development, *we* will focus on the latter.

When it was clear to politicians that the United States would no longer be able to maintain its economic dominance by producing anything industrially valuable or viable, many committees were formed and tasked to come up with the answer to one crucial question: How can the US maintain its global dominance if (or when) it is not producing anything competitively valuable?

The response came from an unexpected direction: Pfizer.

The President of Pfizer, Edmund Pratt, had a furious op-ed piece in a New York Times on July 9, 1982 titled "Stealing from the Mind". It fumed about how third world countries were stealing from them. (By this, he referred to countries making medicine from their own raw materials with their own factories using their own knowledge in their own time for their own people, who were frequently dying from horrible but curable third-world conditions.) Major policymakers saw a glimpse of an answer in Pfizer's and Pratt's thinking, and turned to Pratt's involvement in another committee directly under the President. This committee was the magic ACTN: Advisory Committee on Trade Negotiations.

What the ACTN recommended, following Pfizer's lead, was so daring and provocative that nobody was really sure whether to try it out. The US would try linking its trade negotiations and foreign policy. Any country who didn't sign lopsided "free trade" deals that heavily redefined value would be branded in a myriad of bad ways, the most notable being the "Special 301 watchlist". This list is supposed to be a list of nations not respecting copyright enough. A majority of the world's population lives in countries that are on it, among them Canada.

So the solution to not producing anything of value in international trade was to redefine "producing", "anything", and "value" in an international political context, and to do so by bullying. It worked. The ACTN blueprints were set in motion by US Trade Representatives, using unilateral bullying to push foreign governments into enacting legislation that favored American industry interests, bilateral "free trade" agreements that did the same, and multilateral agreements that raised the bar worldwide in protection of American interests.

In this way, the United States was able to create an exchange of values where they would rent out blueprints and get finished products from those blueprints in return. This would be considered as a fair deal under the "free trade" agreements which redefined value artificially.

The entire US monopolized industry was behind this push: the copyright industries, the patent industries, all of them. They went forum shopping and tried to go to WIPO — repeating the hijack of the record industry in 1961 — to seek legitimacy and hostship for a new trade agreement that would be marketed as "Berne Plus".

At this point, it became politically necessary for the US to join the Berne Convention for credibility reasons, as WIPO is the overseer of Berne.

However, WIPO saw right through this scheme and more or less kicked them right out the door. WIPO was not created to give any country that kind of advantage over the rest of the world. They were outraged at the shameless attempt to hijack the copyright and patent monopolies.

So, another forum was needed. The US monopoly industry consortium approached GATT — the General Agreement on Tariffs and Trade — and managed to get influence there. A major process was initiated whereby about half of the participating countries in GATT were tricked, coerced or bullied into agreeing with a new agreement under GATT, an agreement which would lock in the Berne Convention and strengthen the US industry considerably on top of that by redefining "producing", "thing" and "value". This agreement was called *TRIPs*. Upon ratification of the TRIPs agreement, the GATT body was renamed WTO, the *World Trade Organization*. The 52 GATT countries choosing to stay out of the WTO would soon find themselves in an economic position where it became economically impossible not to sign the colonizing terms. Only one country out of the original 129 has not rejoined.

TRIPs has been under considerable fire for how it is constructed to enrich the rich at the expense of the poor, and when they can't pay with money, they pay with their health and sometimes their lives. It forbids third world countries from making medicine in their own factories from their own raw materials with their own knowledge to their own people. After several near-revolts, some concessions were made in TRIPs to "allow" for this.

But perhaps the most telling story of how important the artificial monopolies are to the United States' dominance came when Russia sought admission into the WTO (for incomprehensible reasons). To allow Russia admission, the United States demanded that the Russia-legal music shop AllofMP3 should be closed. This shop sold copies of MP3 files and was classified as a radio station in Russia, paying appropriate license fees and was fully legal.

Now, let's go back a bit to review what was going on. This was the United States and Russia sitting at the negotiating table. Former enemies who kept each other at nuclear gunpoint 24 hours a day, 7 days a week, through sandstorm and blizzard. The United States could have demanded and gotten anything. Absolutely anything.

So what did the United States demand?

It asked for Russia to *close a bloody record store.*

That's when you realize how much power these monopolies have.

Copyright As A Fundamentalist Religion

What is happening now with the copyright industry vs. the people is practically identical to what happened when the printing press was introduced and the Catholic Church declared war on self-educated people. In both cases, it is not really about religion or law, but about the very simple principle that people are people and that powerful people will use their power to keep their power.

What is interesting here is that copyright defenders are acting like religious fundamentalists. They aren't religious in the actual sense of the word, of course. But they are acting and reacting as if they were religious about copyright, as if it was something that wasn't allowed to be questioned.

Enrique Dans observes that they are attacking not just copyright reformists, but anybody who even questions copyright, with an emotional and aggressive fervor: calling the reformists *pirates*, *thieves*, *freetards* et cetera. In another time and place, *heretics* would have been the word of choice.

Facts and figures that shed light on the situation and could help find a solution to the problem are never welcomed, but are aggressively rejected and ignored by the copyright fundamentalists.

There are a couple of observations to be made from this.

First, people are people and will be people; there's nothing new under the sun. All of this has happened before and will happen again.

The printing press was a disruptive technology that threatened the control over information that the Catholic Church had enjoyed so far. When the old power structures saw the risk of their power slipping away or being eroded, they fought back in every way they could. And although technology won in the end, the former information monopolists managed to create quite a lot of collateral damage to society before they had to accept the inevitable defeat.

The Internet is a disruptive technology that threatens the control over information that the entertainment industry has enjoyed so far. When the old power structures see the risk of their power slipping away or being eroded, they fight back in every way they can. And although technology will win in the end, the former information monopolists are creating quite a lot of collateral damage to society right now.

Our job is to put an end to this damage as quickly as possible, so that society can take full advantage of the new opportunities that technology has opened up. The region of the world that is the first one to achieve this will be among the economic winners of this century.

Second, we are seeing emotional reactions that are identical to that of the Catholic Church when the printing press arrived. Since copyright is religious to these people, there is no middle ground and will never be a middle ground – the concept is as unrealistic as a middle ground between the Quran and the Bible. Again, it should be emphasized that it is not a religion per se, but that the people are reacting as though they were defending their religion. They are deeply, deeply uncomfortable by things being questioned that cannot and must not be questioned, and are reacting by emotional distress and full-on attack.

Third, and most interesting: once this has been identified, we can follow the script for how the Catholic Church was defeated by knowledge 500 years ago, and win again against the religion of these modern no-knowledge-proliferation treaties. One needs to remember that the Catholic Church had instituted excommunication (exile) as penalty for unauthorized reading. They had persuaded France to enact the death penalty for using a printer to produce books. They were really tenacious about preventing the spread of knowledge. In the end, that was also what undid their stranglehold on the populace: that everybody learned how to read, and could question their word for themselves.

So the fight 500 years ago was one against knowledge, and it was won by spreading knowledge.

That's exactly how we need to win today.

We need to **teach the whole world how to share culture.** Everybody needs to *experience* what the copyright industry is trying to kill. We need to connect Aunt Marge's television set to a one-terabyte USB drive of hi-def movies with a media player, just like Protestants won by teaching people to read. Just like you can't un-experience what it's like to read, you can't unexperience what it's like to have the world's culture and knowledge at your fingertips. We need to help everybody around us understand that sharing is caring, and that copyright is the opposite.

We need to **document the transgressions** of the copyright industry. Much sympathy was gained for the Protestant causes as the cruelties of the Spanish Inquisition and Bloody Mary were exposed to the public. There is certainly no shortage of horrendous acts on behalf of the copyright industry. We need to explain them in laymen's terms.

We need to *explain that there is a better way* to both politicians, artists, and citizens in general. Copyright is just a piece of legislation, written by humans, that has developed into something that is out of sync with reality. It is not a holy stone tablet handed down to us directly by God, and it is not an eternal principle that holds our society together. It is just a piece of legislation that happens to be broken, and can be fixed. But it needs to be fixed quite urgently, or we risk creating a kind of society that we do not want.

To conclude:

File sharing is not just a private matter. It's a matter of global economic dominance, and always has been. Let's keep sharing and move that power from the monopolists to the people. Teach everybody to share culture, and the people will win against the constrainers of liberties, just as happened at the start of this series, when people learned to read for themselves and toppled the Catholic Churh.

Chapter 5

The Artists Are Doing Fine

How Will The Artists Get Paid?

"But how will the artists get paid?" is the single most frequent question we Pirates get when arguing for copyright reform to legalize file sharing.

Ten years ago, this was a very difficult question to answer, and few would have been confident that they knew if and how the cultural sector would survive financially in the new era. But today, we have more than a decade's experience of a world where anybody who wants can download whatever they want for free, and where a large portion of the population routinely does.

We now know from experience that **the cultural sector is financially sustainable despite rampant p2p file sharing.** What may have appeared to be an insoluble problem a decade ago, has turned out not to be a problem at all, but in fact a huge opportunity for artists and creators, and a boon for sustainable cultural diversity.

Admittedly, it can feel a bit frustrating to get the question of how the artists will get paid after you have just explained how copyright enforcement is threatening fundamental rights. Should the question of whether we want to keep the right to private communication, due process, and proportionality in punishments really depend on whether it is profitable for artists or not?

But apart from that, it is a relevant question. We all want a society where culture flourishes, and we all want authors, musicians, and other creative people to have a chance to make a living from their art. If it had been the case that there actually was a conflict between this and preserving fundamental rights, it would have been a problem that needed to be addressed, even if abolishing fundamental rights would not have been the proper answer.

As it happens, we can see that during the decade when file sharing grew exponentially, revenues have increased year by year for the both the cultural sector as a whole, and for each individual segment such as film, music, or computer games.

The biggest change has been within the music industry. For the past ten years, sales of recorded music have declined steeply, and the rise in digital music-sales have been scant compensation. But the music business has never been healthier.

In an in-depth article published in October 2010, business magazine The Economist wrote:

> A surprising number of things are making money for artists and music firms, and others show great promise. The music business is not dying. But it is changing profoundly.

> The longest, loudest boom is in live music. Between 1999 and 2009 concert-ticket sales in America tripled in value, from $1.5 billion to $4.6 billion. [...]

> Rising income from live performance, merchandising, sponsorship, publishing, online streaming and emerging markets has come to counterbalance losses from declining CD sales. As a result, some musicians are singing a different tune. Last year a new group, the Featured Artists Coalition, objected to government plans to punish file-sharers by suspending their broadband connections. Its leaders, including established artists such as Billy Bragg and Annie Lennox, argue that file-sharing is a useful form of promotion.

When we look at the statistics, we see that the cultural sector is making as much money now as it did ten years ago (or slightly more, due to the general increase in standard of living). People are spending as much money as ever on culture, regardless of the fact that they can download just about anything for free, and frequently do.

If they no longer spend the money on one thing, they spend it on something else. Music fans are spending just as much money as they used to on music, but since they are spending less on plastic discs, they are spending more on going to live concerts. This is bad news for the record companies, but it is great news for the artists, who get a bigger piece of the pie.

More money than ever before goes into the cultural sector, but sometimes through a different route.

It is quite natural that this should be the case, if we think about our own every-day experience of how an ordinary private economy works. When you get a salary every month, you first spend most of it on rent, food, bills, and other boring things. Then, if you're lucky, you have a little bit left that you can spend on entertainment, i.e.: culture.

If you no longer spend that money on buying plastic discs, you can afford to go and listen to some live music instead. You're going to spend the money one way or another, so someone in the cultural sector will get it.

It is still very difficult to make a living as an artist, it always has been, and it always will be. But at least it has become a little bit easier than it was before the Internet and p2p file sharing. In the music business, total revenues have increased slightly, while the big record companies are getting a smaller piece of the pie. This has left more money for the creative people who actually make the music (rather than just distribute it).

File sharing is not a problem that needs to be solved. It is something that is positive for both artists, consumers, and society as a whole. All we need to do now is to get copyright legislation in line with this new and positive reality.

By reforming copyright to legalize p2p file sharing that is done without direct commercial intent, we can put an end to the criminalization of an entire generation, while at the same time improving conditions for a vibrant cultural sector in Europe.

Studies On The Cultural Sector In The File Sharing Era

There is quite a lot of academic research on how the cultural sector, including the music business, has fared in the file sharing era. These studies make very interesting reading, and should be obligatory reading for all politicians involved in copyright policy making.

First, three studies on the music business in various member states:

• UK 2004 – 2008: Record companies lose, artists gain from file sharing

• Sweden 2000 – 2008: More Charts The Record Labels Don't Want You To See: Swedish Musicians Making More Money

• Norway 1999 – 2009: Artists Make More Money in File-Sharing Age Than Before It

All three studies conclude that although record sales are down, revenues from live performances have increased dramatically, in a way that more than compensates for the drop in sales of recorded music.

The Dutch study *Ups and downs – Economic and cultural effects of file sharing on music, film and games* (2009) takes a combined look at different cultural genres. It shows that between 1999 and 2007, revenues have increased for all of them, except music recordings. For the music industry, this study only looks at recorded music, and does not examine income for artists from other sources, such as concerts. This means that the study only confirms the negative trend for recorded music in line with the Swedish, Norwegian, and UK studies above, but leaves the part of the music sector that has made up for this outside the scope of the study.

A **Harvard study** from 2009 takes a look at the wider implications of file sharing for society, and finds that since the advent of file sharing, both the number of music albums and films released per year have increased. Canadian law professor Michael Geist summarizes the study under the heading *Harvard Study Finds Weaker Copyright Protection Has Benefited Society.*

The Hargreaves report was commissioned by the UK government, and published in May 2011. It makes a strong call for evidence-based policy making in copyright matters, as opposed to having policy determined by the weight of lobbying.

Although the report is by no means a "Pirate Manifesto", it makes several concrete proposals for policy changes that would at least go in the right direction.

The studies that have been mentioned here are summarized in a little more detail in the following sections.

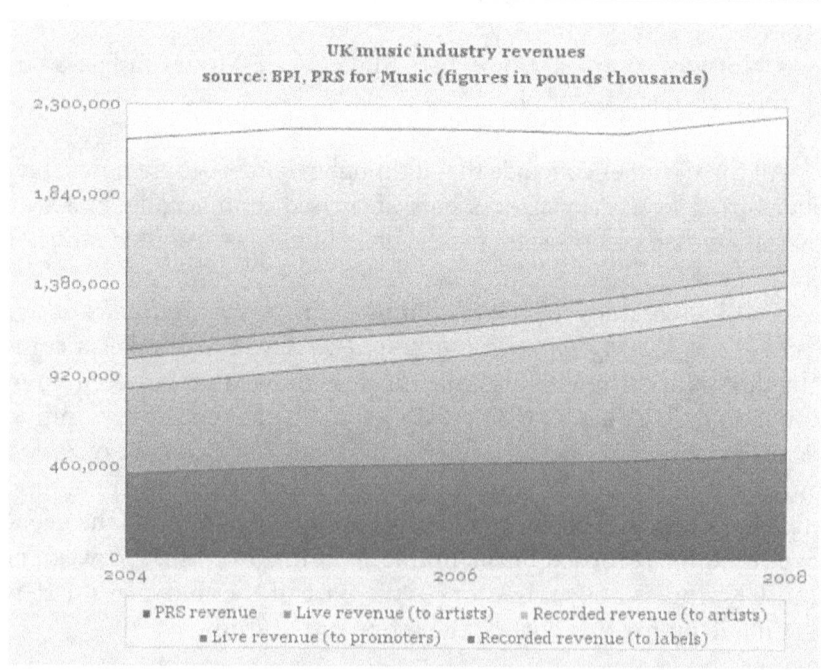

UK music industry revenues
source: BPI, PRS for Music (figures in pounds thousands)

UK 2004 - 2008:
Record Companies Lose, Artists Gain From File Sharing

On the previous page you will find *"The graph the record industry doesn't want you to see"* according to *Telegraph* editor Shane Richmond.

Times Labs has made an analysis of the music market in the UK for the last five years, based on data from the UK collecting society PRS.

In the graph, the top field is what the record companies make. The four other fields are what the artists make. The conclusion is very clear:

Record companies are making less, artists are making more, and the total amount is constant.

The reason record companies are making less money than they used to is probably due to file sharing. We Pirates happy to concede that. File sharing is a much better way to distribute music, so the service that the record companies provided is less and less in demand. It is only natural that they are in decline.

The best thing about this, is that the artists are making more money. People are spending just as much as they used to on music, but the record companies are getting less. Instead, the artists have increased their share to soak up the money that has become available.

This is an excellent development, and something we should embrace. File sharing should be legalized. The artists are the ones who have the most to gain.

Opposite page: Music industry revenues in the UK, 2004 - 2008

Sweden 2000 – 2008:
More Charts The Record Labels Don't Want You To See:
Swedish Musicians Making More Money

Mike Masnick at *Techdirt* writes:

> We've already discussed the research on the UK music indus-
> try that shows both that live revenue is more than making up
> the decline in recorded revenue and that musicians themselves
> are making more revenue than ever before. Some people have
> suggested that this is a UK-only phenomenon, but a worldwide
> study found the same thing as well. And, now it looks like the
> same is being found in Sweden as well – home of The Pirate Bay,
> which we keep being told is destroying the industry. Swedish
> indie record label owner Martin sends in the news on data from
> the Swedish music industry, which looks quite similar to the UK
> data. First, it shows that while there was a tiny dip in overall
> revenue, it's back up to being close to it's high, mostly because
> of a big growth in live music:

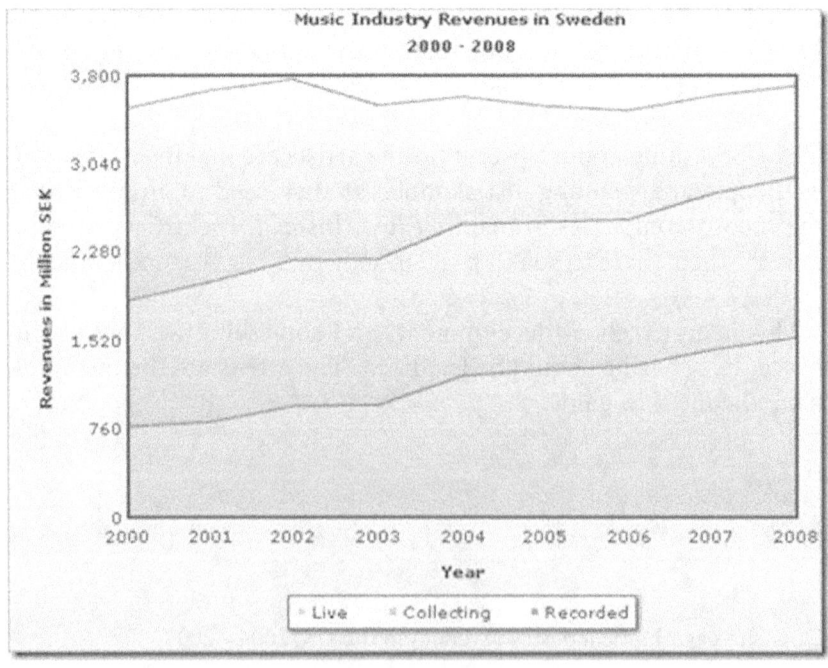

Basically, recorded revenues dropped. Collections stayed about the same, but live grew. More importantly, though, is the second chart, which shows the revenue for actual musicians. And that's going in one direction: up.

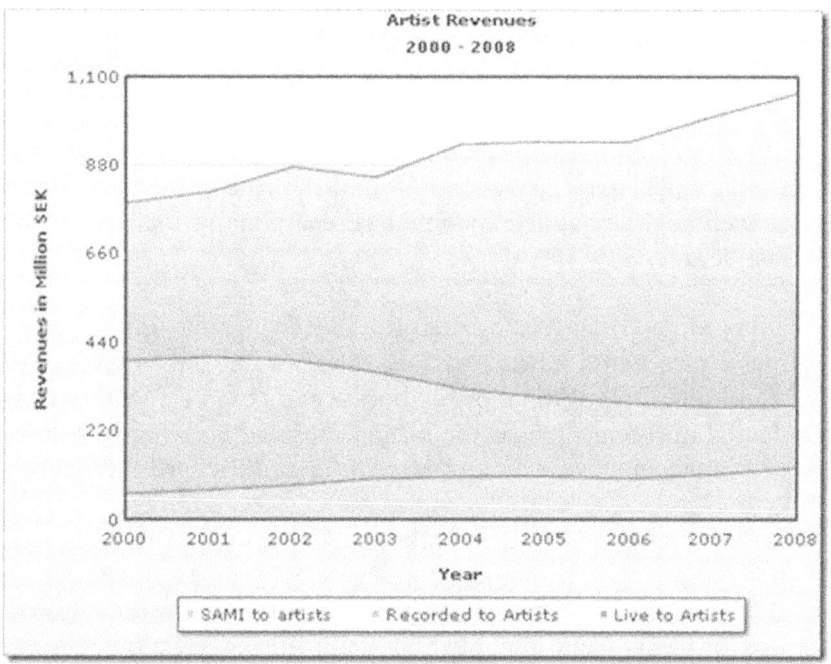

And yet, The Pirate Bay is destroying the ability to make music, right? Funny that the numbers don't seem to support that at all. Basically, these charts are showing the same thing that those other studies have shown. More music is being created. There is greater "discovery" of new music. There are greater revenue opportunities for musicians, and the only part of the business that appears to be suffering is the part that involves selling plastic discs. Yes, that sucks if your business was based on selling plastic discs, but for those who can adapt and adjust, there is more money than ever before to be made. That sorta goes against the claims that "piracy" is somehow destroying the industry, doesn't it?

Norway 1999 – 2009:
Artists Make More Money In File Sharing Age
Than Before It

Ernesto at *Torrentfreak* writes:

An extensive study into the effect of digitalization on the music industry in Norway has shed an interesting light on the position of artists today, compared to 1999. While the music industry often talks about artists being on the brink of bankruptcy due to illicit file sharing, the study found that the number of artists as well as their average income has seen a major increase in the last decade.

Every other month a new study addressing the link between music piracy and music revenues surfaces, but only a few really stand out. One of the most elaborate and complete studies conducted in recent times is the master thesis of Norwegian School of Management students Anders Sørbo and Richard Bjerkøe.

In their thesis, the students take a detailed look at the different revenue streams of the music industry between 1999 and 2009. By doing so, they aim to answer the question of how the digitization of music – and the most common side effect, piracy – have changed the economic position of the Norwegian music industry and Norwegian artists. The results are striking.

After crunching the music industry's numbers the researchers found that total industry revenue grew from 1.4 billion Norwegian kronor in 1999 to 1.9 billion in 2009. After adjusting this figure for inflation this comes down to a 4% increase in revenues for the music industry in this time period. Admittedly, this is not much of a growth, but things get more interesting when the research zooms in on artist revenue.

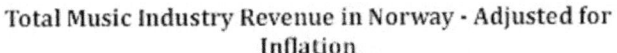

Total Music Industry Revenue in Norway - Adjusted for Inflation

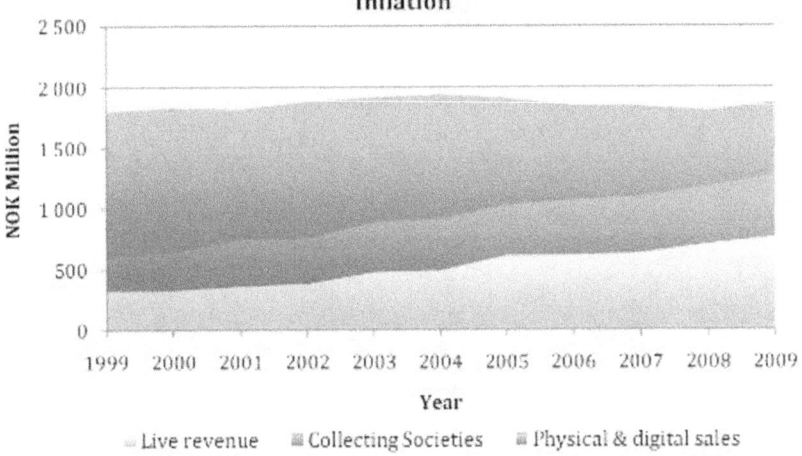

Live revenue   Collecting Societies   Physical & digital sales

In the same period when the overall revenues of the industry grew by only 4%, the revenue for artists alone more than doubled with an increase of 114%. After an inflation adjustment, artist revenue went up from 255 million in 1999 to 545 million kronor in 2009.

Some of the growth can be attributed to the fact that the number of artists increased by 28% in the same time period. However, per artist the yearly income still saw a 66% increase from 80,000 to 133,000 kronor between 1999 and 2009. In conclusion, one could say that artists are far better off now than they were before the digitization of music started.

Aside from looking at the reported revenue, the researchers also polled the artists themselves to find out what their income sources are. Here, it was found that record sales have never been a large part of the annual revenue of artists. In 1999, 70% of the artists made less than 9% of their total income from record sales, and in 2009 this went down to 50%.

Live performances are the major source of income for most artists. 37% of Norwegian artists made more than 50% of their income from live performances in 2009, up from 25% in 1999. That said, it has to be noted that only a few artists make a full living off their music, as most have other jobs aside.

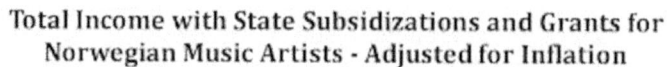

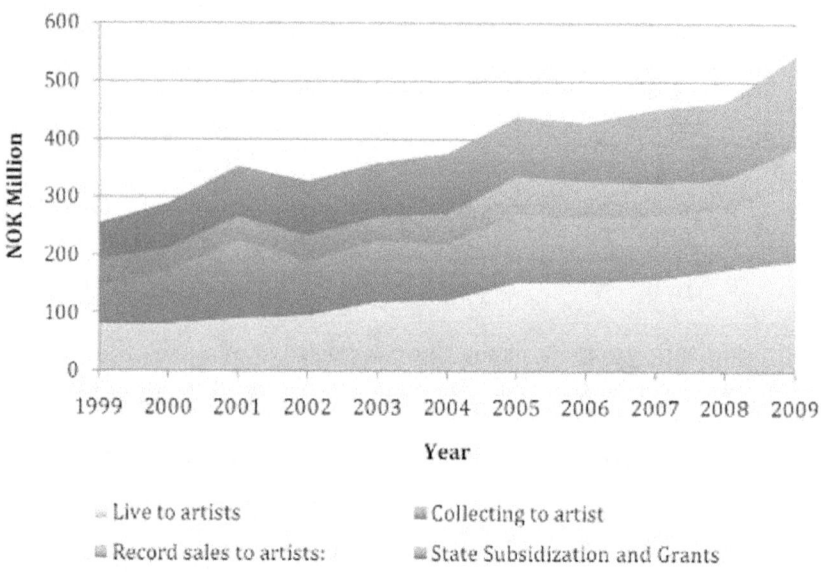

Total Income with State Subsidizations and Grants for Norwegian Music Artists - Adjusted for Inflation

In conclusion, the study refutes some of the most common misconceptions about the music industry in the digital age. Musicians are making more money than ever before. It is true that the revenues from record sales are dwindling, but that can be just as easily attributed to iTunes as The Pirate Bay.

The bottom line is that the music industry as a whole is thriving. Record labels may report a dip in their income from record sales, but more money is going to artists at the same time. Is that really such a bad outcome? Well, that depends on who you're listening to.

Dutch Study:
Ups And Downs – Economic And Cultural Effects
Of File Sharing On Music, Film And Games (2009)

Mike Masnick at *Techdirt* writes:

[This study] is a very long (128 pages), but very thorough research report analyzing pretty much everything having to do with file sharing in the Netherlands, commissioned by the government. It studies the economic angles, the legal angles, the cultural angles – and then compares the local results to international results.

While you might quibble with some of the methodology here or there, the overall conclusions of the report are pretty strong and clear: file sharing is not a problem for the overall industry. File sharing has, in fact, created a net benefit to the economy and society in both the short and long term, and that will likely continue.

The direct impact on sales of file sharing is minimal (though it depends on the category). In fact, the only areas actually in trouble right now may be the sale of plastic discs (CDs and DVDs), but much of the damage has nothing to do with file sharing, and there are indications that the "lost" money can be made up in other ways. The report recommends moving away from criminalizing user activities, and focusing instead on encouraging new business model development. A quick excerpt from the conclusions:

> The short-term net welfare effects of file sharing are strongly positive given that it is practised by consumers whose demand is driven by a lack of purchasing power. To the extent that file sharing results in a decline in sales, we see a transfer of welfare from operators/producers to consumers, with no net welfare effect.
>
> The market for CDs and the market for DVD/VHS rentals are the only sectors of the entertainment industry that are

suffering from a slump in sales. Whereas this may be attributed in part to file-sharing activity, file sharing is not solely to blame for the decline. The markets for DVDs and console games continued grow impressively after P2P services were introduced, and the cinema market showed sustained growth between 1999 and 2007. The total entertainment market has remained more or less constant, suggesting budget competition among the various products.

As long as the markets for games and films are on the rise or remain stable, there is little reason for concern that the diversity and accessibility of content is at stake. File sharing has significantly enhanced access to a wide and diverse range of products, albeit that access tends not to have the approval of the copyright holders.

In other words, pretty much everything that plenty of folks around here have been saying for a better part of a decade is pretty much true. File sharing isn't damaging – and, in fact, can represent a net economic improvement, and the business troubles faced by a few small parts of the industry are really business model challenges, rather than legal ones. The report makes it clear that focusing on legal solutions to dealing with file sharing is a big mistake that tends to only backfire and seems to be totally misdirected.

Harvard Study Finds Weaker Copyright Protection Has Benefited Society (2009)

Canadian law professor Michael Geist wrote in 2009:

Economists Felix Oberholzer-Gee and Koleman Strumpf have just released a new Harvard Business School working paper called File Sharing and Copyright that raises some important points about file sharing, copyright, and the net benefits to society. The paper, which includes a helpful survey of the prior economic studies on the impact of file sharing, includes the following:

1. The data indicates that file sharing has not discouraged creativity, as the evidence shows significant increases in cultural production. The authors note that:

Overall production figures for the creative industries appear to be consistent with this view that file sharing has not discouraged artists and publishers. While album sales have generally fallen since 2000, the number of albums being created has exploded. In 2000, 35,516 albums were released. Seven years later, 79,695 albums (including 25,159 digital albums) were published (Nielsen SoundScan, 2008). Even if file sharing were the reason that sales have fallen, the new technology does not appear to have exacted a toll on the quantity of music produced. Obviously, it would be nice to adjust output for differences in quality, but we are not aware of any research that has tackled this question.

Similar trends can be seen in other creative industries. For example, the worldwide number of feature films produced each year has increased from 3,807 in 2003 to 4,989 in 2007 (Screen Digest, 2004 and 2008). Countries where film piracy is rampant have typically increased production. This is true in South Korea (80 to 124), India (877 to 1164), and China (140 to 402). During this period, U.S. feature film production has increased from 459 feature films in 2003 to 590 in 2007 (MPAA, 2007).

Given the increase in artistic production along with the greater public access conclude that "weaker copyright protection, it seems, has benefited society." This is consistent with the authors' view that weaker copyright is "unambiguously desirable if it does not lessen the incentives of artists and entertainment companies to produce new works."

2. The paper takes on several longstanding myths about the economic effects of file sharing, noting that many downloaded songs do not represent a lost sale, some mashups may increase the market for the original work, and the entertainment industry

can still steer consumer attention to particular artists (which results in more sales and downloads).

3. The authors' point out that file sharing may not result in reduced incentives to create if the willingness to pay for "complements" increases. They point to rising income from performances or author speaking tours as obvious examples of income that may be enhanced through file sharing. In particular, they focus on a study that concluded that demands for concerts increased due to file sharing and that concert prices have steadily risen during the file sharing era. Moreover, the authors canvass the literature on the effects of file sharing on music sales, confirming that the "results are decidedly mixed."

The authors were one of the first to challenge the early claims about the effects of file sharing. Years later, many other economists have followed suit (including the study funded by Industry Canada). This latest paper does a nice job of expanding the discussion, by using the data to examine incentives for creativity and the effects on aggregate creator and industry income.

The Hargreaves Review Of UK IPR Policies (2011)

The UK government commissioned a review of its policies on copyright, patents and other intellectual property rights (IPR), which was presented in May 2011. The review was done by Professor Ian Hargreaves, who holds the Chair of Digital Economy at the Cardiff School of Journalism, Media and Cultural Studies and Cardiff Business School.

The resulting Hargreaves Review (pdf, 130 pages) is very interesting reading.

One thing should be made absolutely clear: The Hargreaves Review is not a "Pirate Manifesto". It is written from a general pro-IPR perspective, and there are many cases where the Pirate Party disagrees with the proposals made, or thinks that they do not go far enough. In particular, the Review offers no solution to the problem of illegal file sharing, other than the usual enforcement/education policy that has failed so spectacularly for at least a decade.

But if we leave that aside, there are many positive concrete recommendations in the Review that deserve to be taken seriously.

Evidence-based policy making is the first thing that the Review calls for. Already in the Foreword, it says:

We urge Government to ensure that in future, policy on Intellectual Property issues is constructed on the basis of evidence, rather than weight of lobbying...

This is indeed an area where there is much room for improvement. In the Executive Summary, the Hargreaves Review states:

The frequency of major reviews of IP (four in the last six years) indicates the shortcomings of the UK system. In the 1970s, the Banks Review deplored the lack of evidence to support policy judgments, as did the Gowers Review five years ago. Of the 54 recommendations advanced by Gowers, only 25 have been implemented. On copyright issues, lobbying on behalf of rights owners has been more persuasive to Ministers than economic impact assessments.

On copyright, the Review first of all advocates a "digital copyright exchange [that] will facilitate copyright licensing and realise the growth potential of creative industries".

Although it would cause no harm if somebody feels like trying to establish such an exchange under today's copyright legislation, it is very doubtful if this would be enough to solve the problem of easy pan-European licensing, and to lay a foundation for Europe as a Digital Single Market.

But there are other very constructive suggestions. The Review states in its Recommendations:

4. Orphan works. *The Government should legislate to enable licensing of orphan works. This should establish extended collective licensing for mass licensing of orphan works, and a clearance procedure for use of individual works. In both cases, a work should only be treated as an orphan if it cannot be found by search of the databases involved in the proposed Digital Copyright Exchange.*

5. Limits to copyright. *Government should firmly resist over regulation of activities which do not prejudice the central objective of copyright, namely the provision of incentives to creators. Government should deliver copyright exceptions at national level to realise all the opportunities within the EU framework, including format shifting, parody, non-commercial research, and library archiving. The UK should also promote at EU level an exception to support text and data analytics. The UK should give a lead at EU level to develop a further copyright exception designed to build into the EU framework adaptability to new technologies. This would be designed to allow uses enabled by technology of works in ways which do not directly trade on the underlying creative and expressive purpose of the work. The Government should also legislate to ensure that these and other copyright exceptions are protected from override by contract.*

All in all, the Hargreaves Review is well worth reading for anyone who takes an interest in IPR policy. Although the Review is written from a UK perspective, most of the reasoning is equally relevant at the EU level and in other member states.

But the most interesting question is of course to what extent the UK government will follow the Hargreaves recommendations. Unfortunately, only a couple of months after the Hargreaves report was published, we all got a sharp reminder of what the political reality still is. One of the strongest and most unequivocal recommendations of the Hargreaves report was not to extend the protection time for recordings from 50 to 70 years, since there would be a deadweight loss to society and no incentivising effect on the cultural sector.

So, what did the UK government do? In September 2011, four months after it got the Hargreaves report on its table, it pushed for a copyright term extension in the EU Council of Ministers, and got it through.

Having the studies is one thing, getting the policy-makers to read them and act upon them is another. But having access to the studies and knowing what they say brings a clear advantage to anybody interested in policy-making in the copyright field.

Chapter 6

More About The Proposal For Copyright Reform

The Proposal Revisited

Let's have a more in-depth look at the proposal that was presented in Chapter 2. This is what the Pirate Party and the Greens/EFA group in the European Parliament propose:

- Moral Rights Unchanged
- Free Non-Commercial Sharing
- 20 Years Of Commercial Monopoly
- Registration After 5 Years
- Free Sampling
- A Ban On DRM

Taken together, these points constitute a proposal for copyright reform that solves 99% or more of the problems today's copyright legislation is causing, while at the same time allowing 99% or more of the business models that are viable today to continue to be viable.

Moral Rights Unchanged

We propose no changes at all to the moral right of the author to be recognized as the author. If you make something, you have the right to be identified as the author of what you made.

This part of copyright is completely uncontroversial. In fact, good etiquette on the net is often more strict on the subject than any copyright legislation.

Bloggers tend to give credit and link back to sources in a way that far exceeds any legal requirement. There are several reasons for this. It makes your blog more trustworthy if you link to sources so that readers can check the background if they want to. It makes the people you link to happy, so they will get more likely to link back to your own blog on some occasion, and perhaps increase traffic. These are good, practical reasons why it makes sense out of pure self-interest for a blogger to be much more generous with giving credit than any law requires.

But there is also the basic human feeling that if you found something that was interesting to you, you want to give something back by showing your appreciation. This is just human nature, and a very positive aspect of it.

The right to be recognized as the author is under no threat on the Internet, and we propose no changes to this part of the copyright legislation.

Free Non-Commercial Sharing

Trying to stop or reduce file sharing through ever harsher legal enforcement doesn't work. File sharing continues to grow exponentially, no matter what repressive means governments are introducing.

If you think it would be good if all illegal file sharing disappeared, please feel free think so (even if the Pirate Party and others disagree). But that does not alter the fact. Limiting file sharing with laws and punishments doesn't work. More of the same won't either. File sharing is here to stay, like it or not.

We should keep copyright, but limit it to when there is commercial intent. All non-commercial copying and use, such as file sharing, should be legalized. We can add this as a limitation in the copyright legislation, in full compliance with the international treaties like the Berne Convention and WIPO Copyright Treaty (WCT).

In Chapter 3, we saw how the attempts to enforce today's ban on file sharing is threatening fundamental rights in the EU and elsewhere, which would be an unacceptable solution even if it worked, which it doesn't, or if the cultural sector was in fact dying, which it isn't.

In Chapter 5, we saw that the artists and the cultural sector as a whole are doing fine despite file sharing (or perhaps thanks to it), so there is no real problem to be solved.

The key to finding a better way for Europe is to separate commercial use from non-commercial.

If copyright is brought back to only cover commercial activities, it will present no major problems to society. There are some adjustments to be made (in particular the unreasonably long protection times), but there are no problems in principle to enforce copyright for commercial purposes.

The reason is very simple. The principle of "follow the money" is enough to enable the authorities to keep track of commercial activities. If an entrepreneur wants to make money the very first thing he has to do is to tell as many people as possible what he has to offer. But if he is offering something illegal, the police will get to hear about it before he has had the time to attract any larger circle of customers. No further restrictions on fundamental rights are necessary. The control systems that are already in place for other reasons are enough to keep track of commercial activities.

But where do you draw the line between commercial and non-commercial?

It is true that there is a gray zone between commercial and non-commercial activities, but this is a problem that the courts have already solved many times in different areas.

We already have a number of different laws that make a distinction between commercial and non-commercial intent, including copyright legislation as it exists today. This is a good thing, since it means that the courts have already established a praxis for determining what is commercial or not.

If you need a detailed answer as to exactly where to draw the line, you should ask a copyright lawyer (and pay 300 euros per hour). This is about how courts interpret the current legislation, and there the lawyers are the experts.

But generally speaking, the line between commercial and non-commercial intent is roughly where you would expect it to be. If you as a private person have a blog without any ads, it's non-commercial. If you get a few euros per month from Google Ads, your blog is probably still non-commercial, since it is a limited amount of money and your primary purpose with the blog is not to earn money from it. But if it is a big blog that generates substantial income from ads, it probably crosses the line and becomes commercial.

There are a number of copyright licenses, including the Creative Commons Attribution-NonCommercial License, that make use of this already existing definition.

Even if it is true that drawing the line can sometimes be a problem, it has already been solved in a reasonable way.

20 Years Of Commercial Monopoly

Much of today's entertainment industry is built on the commercial exclusivity on copyrighted works, and we want to preserve this. But today's protection times – life plus 70 years – are absurd. No investor would even look at a business case where the time to pay-back was that long.

We want to shorten the protection time to something that is reasonable from both society's and an investor's point of view, and propose 20 years from publication.

And we want to have the same protection term for all kinds of works.

Wouldn't it make sense to have different protection times for different kinds of works? 20 years protection for a computer programs probably has different implications than 20 years for a piece of music or a film. Wouldn't it be better to adapt the protection times according to what is reasonable for different categories of works?

This is actually what I (Christian Engström) thought myself, until I discussed it with a friend who agreed completely. When we started talking, we both agreed that it would be reasonable to have different protection times, since the markets work so differently.

I, who have a background as a programmer, thought it was quite reasonable to have a longer protection time for computer programs, since they quite often continue to be useful long after they were written. Code that I wrote in 1984-86 still runs in production today, and continues to generate income for that company. This is something different than a pop song, which at best is popular for a year or so, before it is forgotten to leave room for new songs. This is what I felt.

But my friend, who has a background as a musician (but is now a copyright lawyer, since that is an easier way to make a living), had the completely opposite opinion. He saw computer programs as something that you upgrade at least every second or third year. Programs older than that would have no commercial value, so it ought to be enough with a quite short protection time for computer programs. Music, on the other hand, could very often live forever, so the protection time for music ought to be much longer. This is what he felt.

And this is how it normally is, my friend, who had had similar discussions with other people, told me. For the kind of works that is closest to your own heart, you would normally find it reasonable to have a longer protection time, but shorter for everything else. This is how most people feel, it appears.

For this reason, we would probably not be able to agree about which kinds of works should have shorter or longer protection times. In this kind of discussions, where you are trying to agree on a time limit of x years, it is in the nature of things that all suggestions for values for x tend to be somewhat arbitrary and picked out of thin air. Having to come up with different semi-arbitrary values for each different category of works just makes it more complicated, and reduces the chances of finding a solution that you can defend with objective arguments.

But if you look at the issue from an investor's point of view, things become different. The music industry may be very different from the computer software sector, but they have one thing in common. Money is money, regardless of what sector you choose to invest it in.

When an investor makes the decision to invest in a project in any industry – it may be music, film, computer programs for the mass market, or anything else – he will calculate his business case with a certain time to get a return on his investment. If the project goes according to plan it is supposed to cover its cost and make a profit within x years. If not, it is a failure.

x is always a very small number in this kind of calculations. That somebody would seriously make a business case for a cultural project where the time to payback is more than three years, probably never happens. People who build bridges and nuclear reactors and the like will of course use longer investment horizons, but outside those industries, business cases that are longer than three years are very uncommon in business in general.

This is of course even more so in the cultural sector. Who can predict what will be cool and hip two or three years from now, in such a fast moving landscape as culture. Most cultural projects are expected to pay for themselves and make a profit within a year.

By looking at the protection times from an investor's point of view, we can justify having the same protection time for all works, even though they are different. The purpose of the economic exclusivity part of copyright is to attract investors to the cultural sector. And investors think in the same way regardless of what they are investing in.

The project should pay for itself and make a profit within one or a few years, otherwise it is a failure. The small theoretical chance that the work that you financed turns out to be a timeless classic that continues to generate revenues for decades is a nice bonus chance for the investor, but nothing that has a place in a serious business case.

So why 20 years, and not 5 or 3?

Our suggestion for a protection time of 20 years is a pragmatic compromise. Even if there are sound arguments for why 5 years or even shorter might be enough from society's point of view, many people still instinctively feel that 5 years would be to short, at least in some cases.

And rather than getting bogged down in an unproductive quarrel over what will always remain at least partly arbitrary numbers, we choose to say 20 years.

The important thing is to get away from today's protection times of a human lifetime or more. These long protection times are clearly harmful to society, since they effectively keep most of our common cultural heritage locked away even long after the majority of the works have lost all their commercial value to the rights holder. This is a deadweight loss in economic terms, and an outrage in cultural ones.

If protection times were reduced to 20 years, this would solve most of the problem of "the black hole of the 20th century", and allow librarians and archivists to start the urgent task of preserving the 20th century works that are rotting away in archives by digitizing them. 5 or 10 years would be better from their point of view, but 20 would be okay.

At the same time, 20 years is still enough to support the pleasant (but very unlikely) dream of creating a major hit that becomes an evergreen that generates revenues for decades. If your next project strikes gold and suddenly propels you into the same kind of long-lasting fame that Paul McCartney or ABBA have enjoyed, 20 years will be more than enough for you to become very rich indeed, and never have to worry about money ever again.

Registration After 5 Years

An *orphan work* is a work that is still in copyright, but where the rights holder is not known or cannot be found. It can be a book, a song, a film, or a photo, or any other kind of work that falls under the copyright legislation.

Orphan works present a big problem for anybody who would want to use them. If you just go ahead without getting a permission, you run the risk that the rights holder suddenly turns up and sues you for a large amount. As we all know, courts can be quite prepared to set the damages for even minor copyright infringements to pretty astronomical figures. In many cases, this is simply not an acceptable risk.

But since there is no known rights holder that you can ask for a license, there is nothing you can do about it. No matter how valuable you think it would be to share that work with the world, there is no way to do it without breaking the law and exposing yourself to a great financial risk. The orphan works are effectively locked away by the copyright system.

This is not a small or marginal problem. A large part of our common cultural heritage from the 20th century falls into this category. About 75% of the books that Google want to digitize as part of their Google Books initiative are out of print, but still under copyright.

Even if it is theoretically possible to find the rights holders for many of these books by making a thorough investigation in each individual case, it simply becomes unfeasible when you want to do mass digitization.

And Google Books is not the only project to digitize works and make them available, even if it is the one that has attracted the most attention lately. There is an EU project called Europeana with a similar goal, as well as the open initiative Project Gutenberg. All of these are being held back by the problem of orphan (or semi-orphan) works.

Unless we do something, a large part of our common cultural heritage from the 20th century risks getting lost in a black hole before it becomes legal to save it for posterity.

To reduce the copyright protection time to 20 years would solve most of this problem, but for technical legal reasons, this is unlikely to happen fast. In order to reduce the protection times like this we would have to renegotiate a number of international treaties on copyright, such as the Berne Convention. Although this is something Europe most certainly has the political and economic strength to do this once we have the political will, it will take time to get there even in a best case scenario. We need something that can be implemented faster.

We propose that copyright (including the monopoly on commercial use and distribution) should be granted automatically without registration when a work is published, just like today. But if a rights holder wants to exercise that commercial monopoly for more than 5 years, he should be required to register the work after the first 5 years have lapsed.

Rights holders who have chosen not to register their claim to a work that was published more than 5 years ago would still keep their copyright as such, but would be seen as having waived their commercial monopoly rights by not registering the work.

From a technical legal point of view this is perfectly compatible with the Berne Convention, since this does not alter the *existence* of the right, but merely adds a reasonable and justified condition on the *exercise* of that right.

All we are saying is that if you want money for the use of a work that is older than 5 years, you have to make it known in a public database how to contact you and where to send the money. This is not an onerous or unreasonable demand in any way.

At the same time, the existence of public databases where anyone interested in licensing a work commercially can easily find the relevant rights holders, will of course benefit the rights holders. If you want to sell something, making your identity know to would-be buyers is quite obviously in your own interest.

Registration after 5 years is a win-win proposal that can be implemented quickly and easily.

Free Sampling

In its description of the documentary film *Copyright Criminals*, the US broadcaster PBS writes:

Long before people began posting their homemade video mashups on the Web, hip-hop musicians were perfecting the art of audio montage through sampling. Sampling — or riffing — is as old as music itself, but new technologies developed in the 1980s and 1990s made it easier to reuse existing sound recordings. Acts like Public Enemy, De La Soul and the Beastie Boys created complex rhythms, references and nuanced layers of original and appropriated sound. But by the early 1990s, sampling had collided with the law. When recording industry lawyers got involved, what was once called "borrowed melody" became "copyright infringement."

Copyright Criminals examines the creative and commercial value of musical sampling, including the related debates over artistic expression, copyright law and money. The film showcases many of hip-hop music's founding figures like Public Enemy, De La Soul and Digital Underground, as well as emerging artists such as audiovisual remixers Eclectic Method. It also provides first-person interviews with artists who have been sampled, such as Clyde Stubblefield — James Brown's drummer and the world's most sampled musician — and commentary by another highly sampled musician, funk legend George Clinton.

Computers, mobile phones and other interactive technologies are changing our relationships with media, blurring the line between producer and consumer and radically changing what it means to be creative. As artists find more inventive ways to insert old influences into new material, *Copyright Criminals* poses the question: Can you own a sound?

Today, the answer to that last question is unfortunately yes. The big record companies do claim ownership on individual sounds and very short samples. If you are a hip-hop musician, be prepared to pay hundreds of thousands of euros up-front for the sampling licenses you need if you ever want to make your music available to the public.

This is clearly an unwarranted restriction on the right to create new culture.

Film makers and other artists who want to create new works by reusing parts of existing works face the same problem.

We want to change this by introducing clear exceptions and limitations to allow remixes and parodies, as well as quotation rights for sound and audiovisual material modeled after the quotation rights that already exist for text.

A Ban On DRM

The purpose of this proposal for copyright reform is to get a balanced legislation that benefits society as a whole, including consumers. But having the right to do something according to the law is of little value in itself, unless you also have the practical means to do it.

DRM is an acronym for "Digital Rights Management", or "Digital Restrictions Management". The term is used to denote a number of different technologies that all aim to restrict consumers' and citizens' ability use and copy works, even when they have a legal right to do so.

In his book *Free Culture*, law professor Lawrence Lessig gives an example of an e-book published by the Adobe company. The book was Alice In Wonderland, which was first published in 1865, and where the copyright has long expired. Since it is no longer under copyright, anybody has the legal right to do whatever he wants with Lewis Carroll's text.

But in this case, Adobe decided to set the DRM "rights" for the e-book to say that you could not copy extracts from it, not print pages from it, and not even lend it or give it to a friend.

Blind and visually impaired people, who need to have e-books converted to accessible formats to be able to enjoy them, are often restricted by DRM. Although they have the legal right to convert the books they have bought, the DRM restrictions prevent them from doing so in practice.

Another example is the region coding on DVDs, which prevents you from watching movies that you have legally bought, if you bought it in a different region of the world from where you bought your DVD player.

These are things that you have all the legal rights in the world to do. But that will do you no good, if a company decides to put DRM restrictions on their product that restrict your technical ability to do so. And not only do the restrictions as such make it difficult to exercise your legal rights for a work that you have bought a copy of. The way the law is written today, it is illegal for you to even try.

This is clearly unreasonable. It should always be legal to circumvent DRM restrictions, and we should consider introducing a ban in the consumer rights legislation on DRM technologies that restrict legal uses of a work.

When doing this, we should define "DRM" as "any technical system that restricts consumers from anything that they have the legal right to do". Since there are exceptions and limitations for certain uses (including the right to make private copies) in the copyright legislation of all countries, this definition covers all systems that one would normally think of as DRM.

There is no point in having our parliaments introduce a balanced and reasonable copyright legislation, if at the same time we allow the big multinational corporations to write their own laws, and enforce them through technical means.

Chapter 7

The Cultural Markets
Of The Future

Nobody Asked For A Refrigerator Fee

A hundred years ago, one of the largest employers in the Stockholm, Sweden, was a company named Stockholm Ice. Their business was as straightforward as it was necessary: help keep perishable food edible for longer by distributing cold in a portable format.

They would cut up large blocks of ice from the frozen lakes in the winter, store them on sawdust in huge barns, cut the blocks into smaller chunks and sell it in the streets. People would buy the ice and keep it with food in special cupboards, so the food would be in cold storage.

(This is why some senior citizens still refer to refrigerators as "ice boxes".)

When households in Stockholm were electrified during the first half of the last century, these distributors of cold were made obsolete. After all, what they distributed was the ability to keep food cold, and suddenly everybody could do that themselves.

This was a fairly rapid process in the cities. With the availability of the refrigerator from circa 1920, most households had their own refrigerator by the end of the 1930s. One of the city's largest employers — distributors of cold — had been made totally obsolete by technical development.

There were many personal tragedies in this era as the icemen lost their bread-winning capacity and needed to retrain to get new jobs in a completely new field. The iceman profession had often been tough to begin with, and seeing your industry disintegrate in real-time didn't make it any easier.

But here are a few things that did not happen as the ice distribution industry became obsolete:

No refrigerator owner was sued for making their own cold and ignoring the existing corporate cold distribution chains.

No laws were proposed that would make electricity companies liable in court if the electricity they provided was used in a way that destroyed icemen's jobs.

Nobody demanded a monthly refrigerator fee from refrigerator owners that would go to the Icemen's Union.

No lavishly expensive expert panels were held in total consensus about how necessary icemen were for the entire economy.

Rather, the distribution monopoly became obsolete, was ignored, and the economy as a whole benefited by the resulting decentralization.

We're now seeing a repeat of this scenario, but where the distribution industry — the copyright industry — has the audacity to stand up and demand special laws and say that the economy will collapse without their unnecessary services. But we learn from history, every time, that it is good when an industry becomes obsolete. That means we have learned something important — to do things in a more efficient way. New skills and trades always appear in its wake.

The copyright industry tells us, again and again and again, that if they can't have their obsolete distribution monopoly enshrined into law with ever-increasing penalties for ignoring it, that no culture will be produced at all. As we have seen, equally time and again, this is hogwash.

What might be true is that the copyright industry can't produce music to the tune of one million US dollars per track. But you can't motivate monopoly legislation based on your costs, when others are doing the same thing for much less — practically zero. There has never been as much music available as now, just because all of us love to create. It's not something we do because of money, it's because of who we are. We have always created.

What about movies, then? Hundred-million productions? There are examples of garage-produced movies (and one even has beat Casablanca to become the most-seen movie of all time in its native country: the film *Star Wreck* in Finland). But it may be true that the argument is somewhat stronger with the blockbuster-type cinema productions.

So far, the film industry has been setting new box office records every year for the last decade. For all their doomsday scenarios, they have never done better financially than right now. But, fair enough, perhaps there will come a time when people will become less interested in paying for hundred-million dollar films.

But even if it would be true that movies can't be made the same way with the Internet and our civil liberties both in existence, then maybe it's just the natural progression of culture.

After all, we have previously had operettas, ballets, and classical concerts as the high points of culture in the past. They all still exist, but they are not at the center of mainstream public attention in the way they once were. Nobody is particularly concerned that those expressions have had their peak and that society has moved on to new expressions of culture. There is no inherent value in writing today's forms of culture into law and preventing the changes we've always had.

Everywhere we look, we see that the copyright monopolies need to be cut down to allow society to move on from today's stranglehold on culture and knowledge. Teenagers today typically don't even see the problem — they take sharing in the connected world so totally for granted, that they discard any signals to the contrary as "old-world nonsense".

And they certainly don't want to pay a refrigerator fee.

Cultural Flat-Rate: A Non-Solution To A Non-Problem

Cultural flat-rate, or global license, or a broadband tax to give money to copyright holders, is an idea that has been around for at least a decade, but has never become reality. There is a reason for this. The idea sounds deceptively simple and possibly attractive when you first hear it, but when you start looking at the details to formulate a concrete proposal, you become aware of the problems.

Collecting the money is one thing. You can discuss if it is fair to force people who do not actually download anything to pay anyway, or why businesses should be compensated for technological progress, or details like how to handle the multiple (mobile) Internet connections that a family normally has. But we leave that aside.

It is when you come to how the money should be distributed that the real fun begins.

• *TV and radio play: Giving to the rich*
If you base the payouts to artists on what is being played on TV and radio, most of the money will go to the established artists that are already doing very well. This is how the current system with levies on blank discs and various electronic devices works.

One of the most attractive features of the Internet is that smaller and not yet established acts can reach an audience, even if they are not played on TV and radio. This is the "long tail" effect, and all the small acts together constitute a fair amount of what is being downloaded from the net.

This is the group of artists that most people would want to support, both for the cultural diversity they provide, and simply because they very often need the money. With a cultural flat-rate based on TV and radio play, they will get very little of the money collected. At the same time, their fans will have less disposable income to spend on these artists, since the fans have had to pay the flat-rate out of their household culture and entertainment budget.

The net effect could very well be a system that reduces income for poor artists, and gives the money to the already rich.

The alternative that most flat-rate proponents favor is to instead measure what is actually shared on the net, and base payouts on those numbers. But that leads to other problems.

• *Billions to porn*
35% of the material downloaded from the net is porn. Pornography has exactly the same copyright protection as other audiovisual works. If the payments from a cultural flat-rate system are to be seen as "compensation" for the downloading of copyrighted works, then 35% of the money should rightly go to the porn industry. Do you think that the politicians should create a system?

The point here is not to criticize porn as such. It is a popular form of entertainment, and there is nothing inherently wrong with it. But this does not mean that it requires billions in government mandated subsidies. Throughout history, this is an industry that has amply demonstrated its ability to stand on its own, if that is an appropriate expression in this context.

But if you want to exclude porn from a cultural flat-rate system, you will not only have to create a "European Board of Morality and Good Taste", or some similar mechanism to draw the line between pornography and art. More importantly, you can no longer use the argument that the cultural flat-rate is a "compensation", or has any connection to copyright.

Instead, it becomes random cultural subsidies at best, or an undisciplined money-grab at worst.

• Filling up the networks

It is technically possible to measure what is being shared on the net with a reasonably high precision. Some people have voiced privacy concerns, but in this particular case, that would not be a problem. The measuring only has to be "good enough", so it is not necessary to track every individual download that everybody does. You can fairly easily design a system to collect good enough statistics without invading anybody's privacy.

But the minute you start paying out money based on the download statistics, people will change their behavior. Today, if you like an artist who has released a new album, you will download that album once so that you can listen to it. But if you know that your favorite artist will get money in proportion to how many times the album is downloaded, you realize that you can help that artist by downloading the same album over and over again.

Since it doesn't cost you any of your own money even if you download the album a thousand times, or a million times, we can expect fans to do exactly that. We know that fans really love their idols, and want them to prosper economically. If all you have to do to make that happen is to start a three-line script on you computer when you are not using it for anything else, a lot of fans will.

The only real limit on the total number of "I-want-to-help-my-favourite-artist downloads" will be the capacity of the Internet infrastructure. In other words: With a cultural flat-rate, the net will turn into a permanent gridlock of completely unnecessary traffic, and no matter how much money backbone providers spend on increasing the capacity, it will fill up immediately.

• A revenue stream for virus writers

Computer viruses are a major problem today, despite the fact that it is actually quite hard for virus writers to make any money from their criminal activities. The purpose of a computer virus is usually to install a back door in your computer, to make it part of a so called "botnet" of thousands of computers that the virus writer can take control of at will.

A botnet owner can sell his services to criminals who want to send spam or commit various forms of advanced fraud, but unless the virus writer has connections to organized crime, it is not trivial for him to convert his virus writing skills into hard cash. With a cultural flat-rate system, that changes.

In principle, all the owner of an illegal botnet needs is a friend who has recorded a song that is covered by copyright. He can then order the thousands of computers in the botnet to download the song again and again. Thanks to the flat-rate system, these downloads will automatically result in real money being paid out to the friend who has the copyright on the song.

In its most primitive form the police would perhaps be able to detect this criminal activity and put an end to it, but it is easy to imagine how more sophisticated criminals can elaborate the scheme. The cultural flat-rate system, which would pump out billions of euros per year on the basis of automatic download statistics, would become a very rewarding target for criminals. Writing harmful computer viruses would become a much more profitable activity than it is today.

• *There is no problem in the first place*
There are several other arguments against cultural flat-rate as well, but we'll skip those and go directly to the final, and very positive one:

There is no problem to be solved.

The Internet is a revolutionary technology that changes many of the preconditions for the cultural industries. The task for policy makers and politicians is not to protect old business models or to invent new ones. However, policy makers do have a responsibility for making sure that we have a society where culture can flourish, and where creative people have a chance to make money from what they do.

Ten years ago, when file sharing on the Internet on a massive scale was a new phenomenon, it was perhaps reasonable to wonder if this new technology would impact the market conditions for artists and creators so that they would find it impossible to make money from culture, and worry that cultural production would drastically decrease in society.

Today, we know better. We know that more culture is being created than ever before, and the people who were predicting "the end of music" or similar doomsday scenarios were simply wrong. There is a growing body of academic research showing that artists are making more money in the file sharing age than before it. The record companies lose, but artists gain from file sharing.

It is not easy to make a living as an artist, and it never has been, but the Internet has opened up new opportunities for creative people who want to find an audience without having to sell their soul to the big companies who used to control all the distribution channels. This is a very positive change for the artists and creators, both from a cultural and an economic perspective.

There is no need to compensate anybody for the fact that technological progress is making the world a better place.

This IS The Market, Stupid!

Henrik Alexandersson writes:

> Working with Pirate MEP Christian Engström in the European Parliament, I often come in contact with advocates for Intellectual Property – lobbyists from the film, music and book industry. And one thing almost always strikes me...
>
> *They don't seem to have a clue about what's really going on.*
>
> They don't seem to realize that we now live in an information society with hyper distribution. And if some of them might have

some sort of a clue after all, it seems they think the Pirate Party or Christian himself invented the Internet, free flow of information and file sharing.

(We sometimes respond to that, saying *"No, that was someone much more clever"*. But they really don't seem to catch the subtle humor, nor the message.)

What the Pirate Party does, is "just" to point out what policies are reasonable in our new society.

Billions of people are online. All of them can, at least in theory, connect with each other. And there is often a surprisingly short distance (or few links) between person B and person Q. A thought, an idea, or an application can spread over the world in just a few days. All kinds of data that are on my computer could be transferred to yours. Or to that of a bike repair man in Chile. If it is good and interesting enough.

Some entrepreneurs have got the message. They start net applications, they set up web stores (that often are more successful, the more specialized they are), they start their own media channels and they start projects where people cooperate. In most cases it can be done with very little money. And if they choose, they can address a global market.

The IP-lobbyists from the entertainment industry, on the other hand... They refuse to see or to accept the real world as it is. They are upset, because people don't want to go downtown to a store to buy their products engraved to plastic discs anymore. They go bananas if someone shares the information he or she has bought with someone else. They curse the Internet. They want so supervise, filter and control the flow of information. They want to cut people off from the net. They have no problem making the world a worse place for everybody else – all the entrepreneurs, scientists, students, activists, artists, bloggers, and ordinary people that every day spontaneously fills the Internet with life and creativity.

The IP-lobby does not make any real effort to accept, embrace and make use of our new reality and of the information society. They could, if they wanted. And they could make a lot of money doing so. But so far, they seem unable and unwilling to think outside the box.

Sometimes it's almost amazing. We met with a person from the book publishing sector. That person told us, with a stiff upper lip, that the amount and the multitude of information on the Internet is a problem – as no one can handle the *selection process*, deciding what should be published and not. So... condescending.

An online information society with a multitude of information and hyper distribution *is* the new market. And in many ways it is a much more free market than the old one. You should accept it – or get out of the way.

And let's face it. Some products, business models, concepts and stuff will end up in the trash can – as they don't fit our modern society. And they *should* end up in the trash – making open space for things that are new, profitable, focused on the future, viable and blooming.

No one can tell what tomorrows business concepts will look like. But you don't need to worry. We'll find out, eventually. The market *will* solve that. On its own. There will always be talented people developing new stuff for new markets. You might call it capitalism, spontaneous order, progress, the invisible hand, dynamic effects or whatever you like. But it will be there.

Trust the Force!

Acknowledgements:

Chapter 3:
Monica Horten, www.iptegrity.com:
EU gives notice of 'Net blocking schemes'
Creative Commons CC-NC-BY 3.0

Chapter 5:
Mike Masnick at Techdirt.com:
More Charts The Record Labels Don't Want You To See: Swedish Musicians Making More Money

Ernesto at Torrentfreak.com:
Artists Make More Money in File-Sharing Age Than Before It
Creative Commons CC-SA 2.0

Mike Masnick at Techdirt.com:
Artists Make More Money in File-Sharing Age Than Before It

Professor Michael Geist, www.michaelgeist.ca:
Harvard Study Finds Weaker Copyright Protection Has Benefited Society
Creative Commons CC-BY 2.0

Chapter 7:
Henrik Alexandersson, henrik-alexandersson.se:
This IS the Market, Stupid!
Creative Commons CC0

This book can also be found

as a free e-book

with active links

and colour charts at

www.copyrightreform.eu